ACCLAIM FOR
JUN Q'ANIL

"An elegant exploration of the human drive to find meaning. Any-one interested in self-discovery should definitely read this book."

—*ABILITY Magazine*

"In this gripping story, Jessica Nagler describes her spiritual journey into her Core Being, and her experiences with the people who shared the mysteries of their magical culture."

—John Perkins, author of *The World Is As You Dream It*

"Enchanting, engaging, and richly textured, full of hidden insights and sound understandings awakened by the challenges and triumphs of her journey."

—Ken McLeod, Buddhist teacher,
and author of *Wake Up to Your Life*

"Jessica Nagler does the hard work for us by venturing into the shadows and bringing back a lantern of knowledge that will guide seekers and explorers of all kinds."

—Kristin Hahn, author of *In Search of Grace*

"A masterful tale of one woman's courageous journey into the Mayan spiritual mysteries. Her refreshing honesty and lyrical writing will grab you, hold you, and leave you wanting more."

— Andrea Cagan, author of *Awakening the Healer Within*

"Nagler succinctly and soulfully describes a perilous journey with brilliant dialogue and brave depiction of her own fears and preconceived notions. A baring account of a woman who shed the world to find the most trusted one of all, herself."

— *Tulsa World*

"An engaging narrative into the shamanic worlds of mystery and magic. This book reflects the growing awareness in Western society that we still possess indigenous hearts."

— Hank Wesselman, Ph D., anthropologist and best-selling author of the *Spiritwalker* trilogy

"Jessica Nagler healed major physical pain by exploring her deepest fears. It took immense courage to use pain as a guide, but in doing so she gained an experience that offers support for others who choose to face their own difficult journeys, wherever they may lead."

— Cynthia Wall, LCSW, author of *The Courage to Trust*

JUN Q'ANIL
ONE WHO WALKS THE WAY

∞

JESSICA NAGLER

Cypress House

JUN Q'ANIL: *One Who Walks the Way*
Copyright ©2005 by Jessica Nagler

Cypress House
155 Cypress Street
Fort Bragg, CA 95437
(800) 773-7782
www.cypresshouse.com

Cover design: Christine Thompson
Cover photo: Leland Auslender
Book design: Michael Brechner/Cypress House

Library of Congress Cataloging-in-Publication Data
Nagler, Jessica.
    Jun Q'anil : one who walks the way / by Jessica Nagler.-- 1st ed.
        p. cm.
    ISBN 1-879384-60-4 (pbk. : alk. paper)
    1. Nagler, Jessica. 2. Spiritual biography--United States.
3. Psychotherapists--United States--Biography. I. Title.
    BL73.N34A3 2005
    204'.092--dc22   2004017125

Printed in the USA
2 4 6 8 9 7 5 3

To my parents, for their inestimable support;
To my first teacher, Sanda Jasper, for helping me to see;
And to Todd, for always knowing.

CONTENTS

JUN Q'ANIL

*One doesn't discover new lands without consenting
to lose sight of the shore for a very long time.*

— *André Gide*

Prologue

MYSTERY GATE

The only thing I knew with certainty was that I needed to leave Los Angeles, not because I was depressed or manic or looking to escape, but because some other part of me was demanding a radical change. I wish I could articulate this better, make it less elusive so it doesn't sound new-agey or clichéd, but the fact that I couldn't describe in words what I felt inside was part of the mystery, the pull. I knew only that after a decade of debilitating health problems and intense inward examination, it was time to make a break from my life and devote myself entirely to personal transformation. I left my fiancé, closed my psychotherapy practice, and sold everything I owned, not because I wanted to, but because I needed to relinquish all that was familiar in order to face something unknown.

Disentangling from life wasn't easy—ending a relationship, a career, letting go of possessions—but nothing challenged me like the headaches. These weren't ordinary headaches; they were headaches that made light and sound and heat intolerable; they made it impossible to think or work or see without a cloudy haze; they required me to sleep a dozen hours a day. When the pain was bad, it was as if I was suffocating. I couldn't seem to get enough oxygen to my brain. I remember precisely the morning they arrived: November 1, 1991, the day after Halloween. I awoke feeling like someone had taken a sledgehammer to my skull. When I moved, cerebral fluid seemed to shift from one side of my brain to the other, like a yolk bouncing around the white of an egg. I knew in that sort of murky, dream-like way that I was in trouble, that something was very wrong, that everything was about to change.

Several years and a lot of energy were spent trying to fix the problem. I knew by heart the waiting room décor of all the best doctors in Los Angeles, none of whom could find anything wrong, except to say that I was stressed. I was stressed, they said. I went to bed healthy (though formerly I'd wrestled with an eating disorder, chronic fatigue, anemia, asthma) and awoke the next morning with my head in a meat grinder. Who wouldn't be stressed? Spinal taps and brain scans revealed that I did not have a tumor, nor was I suffering from an aneurysm; still, I was frantic for an explanation. But even back then some part of me knew that my efforts were futile, that no matter how many tests I had or doctors I visited, there would be no easy answer. This crisis would trigger a lifetime investigation.

But first I'd spend a year evaluating the pros and cons of living.

It wasn't that I wanted to die, or even that I had a plan to do myself in. Rather, I couldn't imagine enduring a lifetime of pain. It didn't seem worth it. I remember sitting on my bed one afternoon, head pounding, vision blurry, scheduling doctors' appointments. I was so sick of telling my story, the history of how it all crept up on me, knowing that I'd be out several thousand dollars with nothing to show for it—no answers, no relief. I wanted to give up, but some deeper force in me kept going.

Eventually, I found a way to manage the headaches, mainly through weekly chiropractic adjustments, and I resumed a semi-normal life, including falling in love, but I carried a profound sadness. I'd examine my reflection in the mirror, look past the image and peer deeply into my eyes. If the eyes were the windows to the soul, my soul was clearly weeping.

I couldn't help but feel that the physical, emotional, and spiritual pain were all wrapped up into one, that somehow I'd gotten off track and didn't know how to shift back to center. I struggled to define my relationship with God (I'm Jewish by birth, non-practicing, just neurotic), but didn't feel connected to my roots, or any roots, and this separation also felt like a void. The most difficult aspect was not having someone to talk to. There were therapists, of course, but most of them just sat staring blankly or tried to twist what had happened into something that didn't resonate. I gained insight from reading, meditating, and talking with friends, but there came a point when I knew I needed guidance. That's when a friend gave me the name of a spiritual counselor named Sanda Jasper.

The sign outside Sanda's Pacific Palisades office read, OSANI HOLISTIC HEALTH CARE: ACUPUNTURE, CLINICAL NUTRITION, REIKI THERAPY AND SPIRITUAL COUNSELING. Red geraniums sprouted from window boxes above neatly trimmed hedges outside the front entrance. Inside, the air was redolent of incense and sage. A statue of the Chinese goddess Kwan Yin and a small water fountain stood in the corner.

A tall, slender woman dressed in gray slacks and a cream cashmere sweater entered the room. "Hello, you must be Jessica," she said. "I'm Sanda." She shook my hand and smiled. "I'll be with you in just a minute."

"Sure," I said.

Surprisingly, Sanda looked more like a regular person than a Maharishi-style guru. She stood slightly hunched over, as if nursing a sore back, and tried to call very little attention to herself. I observed with interest as she attended to a few odds and ends behind the receptionist's desk. I might have felt unnerved if it weren't for her kind eyes and reassuring smile.

"Thanks for waiting," she said when she had finished her tasks. "Come on back."

Sanda offered me a cup of tea and motioned for me to follow her into a small adjoining room. I sat on one of two cushy chairs and noticed a few plants and a framed photograph of the Dalai Lama. There was also a massage table covered with a sheet, which I'd later learn was used for energy work. Sanda took off her shoes and lit a candle before settling back in her chair. Even before we began speaking, I knew that I'd found my teacher.

What puzzled and excited me most about Sanda was that she seemed to know me before she knew me. I felt seen in a way I'd never known but had always longed for. It was as if she perceived my total being, not just my body or image or persona, and this felt deeply comforting.

"What is your intention in coming to see me?" she asked.

Although the question didn't surprise me, I was momentarily stunned. What was my intention in coming to see her? How could I explain that I felt haunted by an inner restlessness I couldn't define, that ever since my engagement I'd been suffering from chronic bladder infections, as if my body had rejected my relationship, or that I had headaches that crept in like monsters in the night? "I feel lost," I said finally. "Like I'm missing a critical piece of who I am and what my purpose is, grasping for a memory that's just out of reach. I feel I'm going through the motions, doing what I've been conditioned to do, wasting my life. It's sad, really. I'm here for some guidance."

"Okay," she said. "So that's your intention, you'd like some guidance to explore what's happening. It's important to be able to state your intention, it helps bring awareness to your thoughts, feelings, and actions. When your intention is unconscious, you're at risk of being controlled by your fears."

"How do you mean?" I asked.

"Well, when we're not conscious of what we're doing and why we're doing it, we tend to be more reactive; we operate out of fear rather than from a place of empowerment. An empowered person is a conscious person, who's always aware of her intention in every choice and action."

"Seems like a lot of effort to be aware in each moment," I said.

"You're right," she said. "It takes effort to become conscious. And not only do you need to be conscious of your intention, you also need to know whether your choices and actions are coming from a place of fear or love."

I tried to take in what Sanda was saying.

"I'm not talking about romantic love," she went on, "or the kind of fear that arises at the edge of a cliff. I'm referring to the essential quality of love and fear—love as the energy of wholeness, and fear as the energy of lack."

While I considered myself to be a relatively conscious person, I could think of many areas that were still being controlled by my unconscious fears. I worried about everything—money, success, achievement. I questioned my ability to be a good partner in a relationship, to be less selfish, less controlling. And I was afraid of the unknown.

"I tend to be pretty hard on myself," I said.

"Yes, I got that sense." Sanda's eyes were smiling but her brows furrowed with genuine concern.

"And I get these headaches." I reached up to touch my temples. "They make me feel like my head is in a vise, like someone wrapped cellophane around my brain. I've been to lots of doctors, but none have been helpful, except my chiropractor."

Sanda sipped her tea and curled her feet up under her like a cat. "Do you know much about the energy body?"

"A little," I said.

"Surrounding our body is an electromagnetic, or auric field," she explained, "a transparent field of energy. It is in this field that we register both positive and negative energy, even when our five senses don't. Being conscious of our energy field is part of being multi-sensory, which means that in any given situation we use our intuitive sense and sensibilities, along with our regular five senses.

"Energy configures not only in this field but also from centers, called chakras, that emanate from the body," she went on. "Each chakra holds and emits a specific energetic frequency, influenced in part by our genetic makeup and individual life experiences, as well as our unique soul imprint. The seven main chakras, then, are an energetic reflection of what's going on with our body, mind, emotions, and spirit."

"So it's possible to read energy?" I asked.

"Yes, there's immeasurable knowledge to be gained from developing your ability to read energy; that is, to hone your intuitive skills so you can perceive and translate these subtle energies. Reading energy is very helpful in understanding how to heal past traumas and old wounds, physical or emotional."

"So the headaches —?"

"What's your sense?" she asked.

"I don't know. My body usually tells me when something's

not right; it's sort of the barometer for how I'm doing. Sometimes there's a clear link between my physical problems and life stressors—like I used to get stomachaches when I was anxious—but often, the connection isn't so clear, though I know it exists."

"Exactly," she said. "That's something we can work on."

"But the headaches are such a mystery," I said. "Especially how they just appeared one day and have never gone away."

"Often it's the greatest mysteries that help us to awaken," she said, "so it's useful to approach things holistically and to view the same situation from many different perspectives. Just as you've gained insight from doctors and healing practitioners, it's important to investigate from within yourself. Becoming conscious of your energy is part of this process. Like right now, are you aware of what your energy is doing?"

"I'm not sure." I knew how to sense other people's energy. Ever since I was a kid I could sense things that others didn't, for instance when someone was camouflaging an emotion; sometimes I even knew what they were thinking, but it hadn't occurred to me to tune in to my own.

"Let me give you a clue," she said, smiling. "If your physical body was doing what your energy is doing right now, you would have me pinned against the wall."

"Oh. I didn't realize I was being so intense."

"It's okay," Sanda laughed. "You didn't mean any harm and I'm capable of handling it, but it's important to know how to manage your energy. It'll help you tremendously."

"How do I do that?" I asked.

"It's a process, like anything else. It doesn't happen immediately. Start by setting the intention to call back your energy. Try it right now and see what happens."

I closed my eyes and tried to tune in to my energy field. It was subtle, but I could feel a slight pulsing sensation around my physical body. Then, because Sanda had said my energy was extended out beyond my field, I tried to pull it back in, focusing on the pulsing sensation until I felt myself more contained.

"That's it," she said. "Your energy followed your intention. You've just taken a step toward becoming conscious on a subtler level."

Over time, Sanda would teach me how to reconfigure my energy, a conscious process of changing the way I thought, felt, and behaved toward myself and the rest of the world. "It can feel awkward, even painful," she had said, "when you shed layers of fear and give birth to something new. It's a kind of spiritual breakthrough that in the beginning can feel like a breakdown."

All this information would take me years to digest and assimilate on all its various levels. Eventually, living more consciously would become second nature, but initially this process was like learning a new language—and indeed I was. And so it went, as Sanda began to clarify and put words to things that I had always felt, but never understood.

1997 was the year of El Niño. Large yellow tractors swarmed the gray beaches, digging trenches, building blockades, trying to safeguard against the inevitable destruction of Mother Nature. A heavy downpour was slowly eating away at the cliffs of the Santa Monica Mountains when I entered Sanda's office and helped myself to a cup of tea. I wrapped myself in a blanket and settled back in my chair, anxious about my upcoming departure.

At this point I'd been working with Sanda for nearly two years. She'd assisted me through family crises, a roster of doctors, a career change, and the profound sadness of breaking my engagement. But it was just the beginning. Now I could see that all those things needed to happen in order to free up enough energy for what I'd always sensed was coming, as if I had to prove to the universe that I was ready. Honestly, I would have preferred just to shift things around a bit, get a little more comfortable, and basically keep my life intact, but such comfort was no longer possible. Instead I felt compelled to leave everything behind and go on a sort of spiritual quest.

I found a small retreat center in the Costa Rican rainforest—it seemed like a good place to get oriented, a landing pad. From there I'd play things by ear. Playing things by ear wasn't my forte, I was more a Type-A control freak, but Sanda explained that this type of journey was about strengthening my ability to trust and allowing things to unfold. Much later I'd see the grace in this way of being, walking in faith instead of by sharply focused sight, but initially it was one of the most difficult lessons to learn.

Once, I asked Sanda why surrender was so difficult.

"Your rational mind, or your executive self," she said, "is like a well-developed muscle. Whenever you have to make a decision or take action, especially when it involves something new, this aspect of yourself naturally takes control. It's the muscle you've come to rely on, it's how you've survived."

I knew I needed to build up my intuitive muscle now; it was time.

I began the process of packing up my things, sorting through and cleaning out everything I owned. Oddly, never had anything felt so right. I said goodbye to my clients, making sure that each one would be taken care of by a new therapist. I completed my last few sessions with Sanda, though we wouldn't really be ending our work. I knew that in some ways I'd be taking her along.

She gave me one of her personal meditation stones to carry with me. "When you need to," she said, "use this in your meditation to connect with me. But remember that you don't actually need anything tangible. Our true connection transcends not only the physical, but space and time as well."

During our last session, when we were discussing some of the potential challenges that lay ahead, she said, "Don't worry, when we need to connect, we will. If we don't connect, know that whatever is happening is a lesson you need to learn on your own."

I smiled tentatively.

"Have a good journey, Jess," she said. "I'll see you on the other side."

SAMADHI

Security is mostly a superstition.
It does not exist in nature, nor do the
children of humans as a whole experience it.
Avoiding danger is no safer in the long run than outright exposure.
Life is either a daring adventure or nothing.

— Helen Keller

Chapter 1

LOOKOUT MOUNTAIN

At dusk there is a golden brilliance to the sky on the Caribbean coast of Costa Rica. The mountainous jungle comes down to kiss the sea, separated only by crooked palm trees and a narrow stretch of sand that tries to be a beach. Clumps of the coral reef protrude even at high tide, and flecks of light play on the water as the sun ducks behind the mountains. A newly paved single-lane highway traces the coastline all the way south to Panama.

Five hours outside of San Jose, on a bus heading to a destination in the remote jungle of the Talamanca Mountains, I drifted in and out of sleep. I was sandwiched between two young surfers, one from Italy, the other from France. The rest of the passengers were Ticos, a nickname the Costa Ricans have given themselves. I swayed with the rocking of the bus, watching the darkness close in, feeling myself drift from self-doubt to excitement and back to self-doubt again. Tucked in my pocket was a torn piece of paper with the name of my stop written in Spanish, which I would hand to the ayudente (bus driver's helper) after we passed a little town called Caquita. My first destination was Hone Creek, known as the ghetto of the Caribbean. There, someone would drive me up the mountain to Samadhi, where I'd begin the first leg of my journey.

One of the surfers nudged me awake, indicating the bus was approaching Hone Creek. In a few minutes, I was alone with my backpack and two seventy-five pound pieces of luggage, standing by the side of the road in the dark. I watched the bus's red tail-lights fade out of sight. There were no signs, no one else wait-ing, and no little bench to denote an official bus stop—just an empty road and jungle all around. I stared intently in all direc-tions. There were sounds I couldn't identify. Were those mon-keys, bats, locusts? I started to feel uneasy. Maybe I'd gotten off at the wrong stop. I thought about flagging down another bus or hitchhiking. But then, where would I go? I was alone in the middle of nowhere.

Not knowing what else to do, I sat down on one of my suit-cases and waited. I was afraid.

Headlights approached on the deserted road, and a 1969 Land Rover came to an abrupt stop right in front of me. A dark, curly-haired man with unnaturally white teeth got out. "You Yessica?" he asked. I nodded. At least now I wouldn't be found dead on the roadside. After loading my baggage, we headed directly up the mountain, which was so steep at times we rolled backwards, even with four-wheel drive. My anxiety continued. The farther up we drove, the more claustrophobic I felt. What if I wanted to leave this place? What if an emergency required a quick getaway? At each bend in the road I prayed that we'd finally reached our destination, but the man kept on driving. I tried to register everything: the fear, excitement, curiosity, and all the other emotions flooding my mind. The stars were luminous and the jungle was thick all around. There was no sign of civilization as far as I could see, until my driver pointed up to the top of the mountain toward a small cluster of twinkling white lights. "Eso es Samadhi!"

He dropped me off at the front office, part of a main structure that housed a large open-air dining room built of wood and surrounded by jungle. I looked around for some form of life, but no one occupied the front desk and the dining room was empty. The gentle sound of flute and percussion music floated through the air, which ordinarily would have calmed me, but in this moment did not. I wondered if it was too late to jump back into the truck and head straight to the airport; I could probably make it home in less than twenty-four hours. Breathe, I reminded myself. Just breathe.

I glanced at my luggage, which was leaning against the railing, and then I looked back to the empty desk. I felt suspended between two worlds: the known, represented by my collection of things, and the unknown, symbolized by the eerie emptiness. How long would I be extracting symbolism from things—the luggage, the railing, the vacant space? Already I missed the carefree nature of a normal vacation, the thoughtlessness of tossing down suitcases and running off to play. But this trip wasn't a vacation; it carried a burden, a seriousness I hadn't expected. What had I expected?

A young girl with dark skin and black braided hair emerged from the kitchen. She greeted me and maintained fleeting eye contact as she picked up a walky-talky and radioed someone in Spanish. I searched her eyes for some sort of recognition, something familiar, hoping she'd confirm I was indeed in the right place, but she didn't speak English. You'd think I would have felt better having arrived safely at my destination, seeing other people, knowing I'd have a bed to sleep in. But I didn't.

Oblivious, of course, to the internal turmoil of her guest, Harriet (silent H) grabbed a flashlight to guide me through the forest to my room.

Minutes later we stopped at a low rectangular building where she flipped on a dim light to reveal a tiny cell-like room with two cots, one window, and no bathroom. A cockroach scampered across the curtains. "There must be a mistake," I said. "I reserved a bungalow overlooking the sea, not a room the size of a jail cell." Immediately, I felt a sharp stab of regret, amazed at how easily I was knocked off center, how quickly I complained without thinking.

Harriet could tell I wasn't happy, but we couldn't do much in the way of talking. I thanked her for showing me the room, deciding to speak with someone else later, hopefully someone who spoke English.

Feeling edgy, I grabbed a towel and rinsed off in one of the communal showers before making my way to dinner by flashlight. The gravel crunched beneath my feet as I followed the road that ran throughout the immense property, providing access for a few old trucks and cars. Clusters of various-sized cottages and bungalows were sprinkled over the mountain. Possibly some were houses. On the way I passed one of my suitcases, forgotten in the dirt road. A few people passed by and laughed at the sight of this lost suitcase. I wanted to explain that I'd been assigned the wrong room, that my suitcase and I were in transition, but I just kept walking.

The dining hall was the central meeting place for the retreat center; it housed the offices and supply rooms and one public bathroom. The area was neat and clean, with beautifully polished wood floors and high-beamed ceilings. Tiny white lights encircled the railing that jutted out over the mountain, and a few wood-bladed fans turned at the ceiling. It was obvious that a great deal of care had been taken to create a pleasant atmosphere, but I still felt unwelcome. I asked a young woman if I could join her table. She nodded that it was okay, but her body language and energy said, "Stay away," so I found another place to sit. I engaged in idle chatter, trying desperately to connect, embarrassed by my own discomfort at being alone.

After dinner I brought my tea down to the lower deck beneath the eating area, and sat under the night sky. The moon had broken through a crack in the clouds and I stared out toward the horizon. I could feel my fear escalating, like a transparent blanket suffocating my consciousness, and I couldn't remember why I'd come. I had a comfortable life back in the U.S.—career, relationship, family, identity—why did I have to go to such extremes? Maybe I would just stay a few days and then go back home. But what would I go back to? I no longer had a house, a job, or a fiancé. The gravity of my situation began to sink in.

My mounting panic was interrupted when Zina, the retreat director, came down to greet me. A petite woman with a reserved smile and a somewhat militant air, she shook my hand and welcomed me to Samadhi. Thankfully, she spoke English.

"You made it," she said. "How was your trip?"

"Long," I said, cupping my hands around the tea mug. Heat vapors tickled my face. "I can't believe I'm here."

We briefly discussed my accommodations, and she said she would try to work out a room change as soon as possible. I wondered if she meant it. Zina seemed to sense my unease, which I know wasn't hard since I practically attached myself to her arm, as if clinging would provide me a bit of comfort. She offered me some herbs to take before bed. "The first night in the jungle can be very, um, different," she said, "if you know what I mean."

Sanda, though, had encouraged me to leave all sleeping aids behind, assuring me that I needed to handle my anxiety in a more conscious fashion. Zina sensed my hesitation, her eyes lingered a little too long, and I found myself wondering why I felt uncomfortable in her presence.

"Thanks," I said, taking the little pouch of pills and tucking them into my pocket.

Zina said good night and I sat awhile and watched the clouds close over the moon, the stars radiant in the inky sky.

When I returned to my cell I surveyed all of my things. Why did I bring so much stuff? Who was going to wear all those clothes, read all those books, take all those medicines? I sat down on one of the little cots and listened to the noises of the jungle. The creatures seemed to be monstrous, as if from some prehistoric land, and the monkeys howled like dogs.

I sat there, in a country where I didn't speak the language, and wondered if I was in trouble. I had just given over $5,000 in traveler's checks, my passport, and my return airline ticket to a woman who spoke no English. She had stapled everything into a torn manila envelope, which she placed in a plywood cabinet, promising that it would be locked in the retreat safe the following day. There was no phone or any other means of outside communication. I'd been told that all written correspondence from the States was delivered to their San Jose office and took an additional week or two to arrive on site. I was at the mercy of these people to take me up and down that ridiculous hill, the same people who had put me in a tiny cell, left my valuables in a plywood cabinet, and failed to orient me. I was alone.

Still, despite the awkwardness and absurdity of my situation, I felt a sense of peace. Nothing was right, yet, in a strange and indescribable way, everything was perfect. I was in the midst of a crash course in trusting the inner wisdom that had unhooked me from my life and brought me here. The question was not whether I had done the right thing, but whether I could allow this experience to unfold without interfering. I had created my fantasy and it scared me.

Chapter 2

CULTIVATING ATTENTION

Awakened at dawn by the sound of howler monkeys making a racket, I went to the window. A tangerine sky had risen over trees changing to deeper shades of purple. Palm fronds rustled in the morning breeze, the air redolent of decaying vegetation and damp earth. The monkeys weren't visible, but the sound of a lute filtered through their screeching, drifting from somewhere in the jungle.

Without changing my clothes or washing, I walked slowly through the forest, almost in a trance, searching for the source of the music. Birds chirped, monkeys screamed, and twigs and branches snapped beneath my feet, but the backdrop of stillness seemed to overpower all sound. It felt eerie to be wandering through the woods in my pajamas, following a strange sound, no particular destination in mind. I smiled at the image of twenty sleeping retreatants being summoned by the sound of a lute, to perform some bizarre ritual in the middle of the rainforest. My imagination seemed to have grown overnight.

As I walked, I took in the forest—the ancient trees, humid

climate, the peek-a-boo expression of a white-faced monkey hiding on his branch. A violet butterfly with about a six-inch wingspan fluttered around me and moved deeper into the foliage. At first I didn't notice the huge octagonal meditation hall standing in the dense forest. Built entirely out of the local cristobal wood, the structure looked at home in its surroundings. The butterfly seemed to hover near the entrance. When I entered the hall, I spotted Zina sitting alone in the dark, eyes closed, peacefully playing her instrument. The moment was so intimate, it felt as if I were trespassing in someone else's dream, and I wasn't sure if I should stay. I couldn't pull away, though, so I stood motionless in the door frame, captivated by the music. When she finished her piece, Zina opened her eyes and gestured for me to enter. She resumed her playing while I sat quietly and listened, calm in the morning, in my surroundings.

Samadhi is situated on 300 acres of virgin rainforest. Other than a few houses and buildings, there is nothing but dense jungle in every direction. Later that first day I wandered around and got lost, not realizing what it meant to be in a real rainforest. It was damp and cool in the bowels of the jungle; elaborate spider webs hung amid the massive trees that formed a giant canopy above. Splinters of sunlight funneled down through the overhang, spotlighting an army of leaf-carrying ants building their colony. The deeper in I walked, the more the surroundings seemed like a living, breathing entity capable of swallowing me whole. I re-emerged around dusk, worn-out and parched, covered in cuts, bruises, and mosquito bites.

The retreat center had an Eastern bent—Buddhist, maybe Hindu—but Samadhi was not a teaching facility. There were no set classes, no formal instruction, and no gurus. I had a place to sleep, food to eat, and a meditation hall at my disposal, but the rest was up to me. I knew this would force self-reliance, which was the point, but right now I felt lost, wishing desperately and a bit sheepishly for someone to tell me what to do. All my extensive preparations seemed elementary, as if they held no weight in the jungle, and I seemed to have forgotten everything Sanda had taught.

On day two, I headed straight to the meditation hall, where again I met up with the purple butterfly, to do yoga and to meditate. I had been practicing yoga for years, and it had become a solid anchor and an entry way into the inner world. When I first decided to take this journey, I knew that maintaining a strong yoga and meditation practice would be essential—I hoped it would provide a sense of calm whenever I wasn't.

Now here I was, sitting in this huge hall, surrounded by jungle, listening to an orchestra of insects, wondering how I would survive the week.

Before leaving Los Angeles I had promised myself that if at any point along this journey I had the inclination to flee, I would wait at least one week before acting. I wanted to ensure that I made a conscious decision rather than reacting out of fear. Here was my first opportunity to honor this promise. I tried to meditate, but my mind was restless and my body ached. I lacked the discipline to continue. I held onto Sanda's stone to help me gain strength, but it didn't help. Instead, I returned to my room, tore open my guidebooks, and ruminated about where else I could go. Anyplace would be better than where I was.

By the end of the week I was beyond frustration. My meditation was erratic, my yoga ineffective, and my desire to go home intense. I was being eaten alive by mosquitoes and other insects, the rain was fierce and had lasted for days without a break, and the constant dampness and humidity of the rainforest seemed to irritate my skin. My normal ringlet curls had become a mass of frizz and I was sick and tired of sharing my shower with frogs and spiders. I still lived in a cell, without decent lighting to read or a desk on which to write. Worst of all, my head was hurting. As a last resort, I decided to talk to Zina.

Born in Italy, Zina had studied in India for ten years before opening the retreat center with three others. In her late thirties, she was pleasant looking, with kinky brown hair and pale eyes. Her nose crinkled when she spoke, and her mood was unpredictable. I found her in the office, a little open niche above the dining room with a 180-degree view of the Caribbean. This was supposed to be my view. The room was furnished with a large desk, a few green director chairs, and a long wooden bench. Zina was sorting through some paperwork when I cleared my throat, announcing my presence.

"Yes?" she said.

"I wondered about my room change," I said. "Is it going to happen anytime soon?"

She looked up and slowly put down her papers. "Are you having a hard time adjusting?"

Was it that obvious? I wanted this to work, had imposed tremendous pressure on myself to get it right, but I felt really overwhelmed. "I had no idea the transition would be so difficult," I said, feeling disarmed.

"Most people aren't prepared for how hard it is to go into retreat, to face themselves without all the distractions of life, never mind being in the jungle. It's a brave thing you're doing, spending this time alone."

I voiced all my complaints—the room, the bugs, the absent sea view. I told her that maybe this wasn't the right place for me after all.

"Maybe," she said. "But I think you're going about it all wrong. You're distracting yourself from what you came here to do."

"How do you know?" I asked.

"You're looking for perfection," she said. "You think if you get everything right, the right room, the right food, the right location, you'll be able to settle down and meditate. But that way of thinking is part of the problem."

I knew she was right. I was very busy focusing on what wasn't right with my surroundings, but was too embarrassed to admit it.

"I can give you another room," she said, "that's not a problem. And I can talk to the kitchen to see if they can better accommodate your diet. But Jessica, life is rarely just the way we want it. The point of spiritual practice is to find a way to be at peace, even when things aren't exactly right."

Everything she said was true, but I hated hearing it. More accurately, I hated that I still had such strong attachments and aversions to things. Zina came and sat down next to me on the wooden bench, obviously aware that I was being hard on myself.

"Being judgmental isn't helpful either," she said. "What you're doing isn't easy. Give yourself a break."

"Do you have any suggestions?" I asked. "I could use some help."

"Well, I can tell you lack discipline."

"I'm very disciplined," I snapped.

"See how easily you become irritated?" she said. "My words shouldn't have that much power over you. You may be disciplined in some areas, even pretty good at observing yourself in others, but in terms of having control over your mind, you're lazy."

"I'm here, aren't I?" I could hear the tone of my voice rising a notch or two. "How many people do you know who've sold everything, closed a successful business, and said goodbye to their lives? What's lazy about that?"

"Yes, you have courage," she said. "And that's important. But you're still attached to your comforts, you need things to be a certain way in order to be happy. You won't find peace if it depends on outward conditions."

I was trying to control my anger, but Zina could see right through me.

"Take a deep breath," she said calmly.

"I already know about that."

"Okay, but do it wholeheartedly," she said. "Right now—stop talking and take a few breaths. Feel the rise and fall of your abdomen, feel the breath pass through your nostrils. Just experience breathing. Then notice what's going on around you, what you're feeling, what's going on in your body. Stay with it a minute."

Taking several deep breaths, I felt my body begin to relax, unwind. I became aware that my breathing was shallow, my neck tense. I described this to Zina.

"Okay good, now open to that."

"What do you mean?" I asked.

"Use the breath as a base of attention, then expand your awareness to include the sensations in the body," she said. "Experience your shallow breathing. Where do you feel it in your body? Your chest? Your throat maybe? What about the tension in your neck? What's that like? Instead of shutting down, be curious. Open to all these sensations, include them in your practice."

"What about when I get distracted?" I asked.

"As soon as you notice you're lost in distraction, bring your attention back to the breath. Don't beat yourself up, it's a waste of energy; just return to the breath and start over."

"I thought I knew this stuff," I said. "I shouldn't be having so much trouble."

"You're in a whole new league now, being on retreat for an indefinite amount of time. Sometimes we need reminding. Don't get tangled up in what should be happening, just experience what is happening—the restlessness of the mind, the aches of the body, the craving to go home, the aversion to staying and everything else. Then return to the breath. This will help to cultivate attention, which will allow you to see more clearly. Give it a try and let me know how it goes," she said, waving an arm in dismissal.

"Thanks," I said.

"Don't mention it."

Over the next few days, as I meditated and went about the daily activities, I noted the running commentary of my mind and where the thoughts went. For instance, during yoga practice I became aware that I was troubled about money and how I could conserve. In the next pose, I started to worry about whether I was going to miss lunch and how I would survive until the next meal. In fact, maybe I should skip lunch, I thought, just to prove that I'm not a prisoner to food. Then I thought about Zina and wondered about her life in India. Before I knew it, I had constructed a scenario about her. I wasn't practicing yoga at all, I was drowning in a sea of thoughts.

I quickly became aware of the harsh critics in my head, the fears that had been controlling my life, and the voices that told me I wasn't enough. I wasn't doing enough, intelligent enough, making enough money, wouldn't amount to enough, wasn't "enlightened" enough and so on. I saw how much energy I was devoting to self-criticism, and it reminded me of my eating-disorder days when I had spent every waking moment thinking about food.

This would give anyone a headache. I started to scold myself, but remembered Zina having said not to judge, just to notice and return to the breath.

The next morning I awakened scratching my body. I threw back the sheets to find I was covered in little red welts, maybe a hundred or more, which I later learned was the result of a no-see-um invasion.

"What are no-see-ums?" I asked Zina later that day.

"They're tiny transparent insects that live in the rainforest. Sometimes they congregate in the rooms and feed on whoever's there. It's very uncomfortable."

"You're telling me?" I said. "I'm ready to crawl out of my skin."

"Use your discomfort to strengthen your practice," she said. "See if you can rest with the breath and open to the itching sensation at the same time."

"You're kidding, right?" I knew she wasn't.

"Every challenge gives you the opportunity to increase your attention," she said, "and to see things more clearly."

"I'm seeing things very clearly," I said. "I have a hundred welts covering my body and it's driving me nuts."

"Yes, your skin itches, but that's a physical sensation that will arise and eventually pass away. It's possible to sit still and experience the itching sensation, but not react to it. There are stories of yogis living in India who remain perfectly still while sitting on hot coals. Of course this requires tremendous mind concentration and I'm not suggesting you try it, but it's possible. My point is, the more you cultivate attention, the less you become a prisoner to the reactive mind, and the more clearly you'll see into the nature of all things. This skill cannot be underestimated."

Though I felt inclined to wallow in my misery, I tried to meditate instead, resting with the breath, trying not to itch,

observing my desire to run out of the meditation hall screaming. It was a lot of work, but after a week of sitting, sometimes
several hours a day, something began to shift. I settled into a
quiet space inside myself, where I was able to observe the endless stream of distractions, but not get lost in it. I was seeing
clearly, for the moment.

I told Zina about my experience. I wanted to sustain this
blissful state, to remain forever the observer, detached from the
thoughts and worries that usually consumed me.

"Don't be seduced by the peacefulness either," she said. "Just
experience what arises and return to the breath. It's easy to
become attached to the more pleasant mind states, but that's a
trap too. I once knew a man who spent two years trying to recap-
ture a certain state of mind, unaware that he was just caught in
another form of attachment."

"You don't give me much to hang on to," I said.

"That's exactly the point," she said. "There's nothing to
hang on to because everything is impermanent. Whether they're
pleasant or unpleasant, all sensations arise and pass away. Any
sense of peace comes from recognizing this."

The more I sat and observed, the more clearly I saw how I
worried about everything—what time I should get up, what I
would eat, how long I should meditate, whether these people
liked me, and did I fit in. The degree of self-absorption was
embarrassing. I felt like I was going backwards, and mentioned
my concern to Zina.

"You're not going backwards," she assured me. "You're seeing what's there more clearly. Your mind is beginning to pene-
trate the deeper layers of your conditioning. This is necessary
before real change can occur."

It was painful to see how much energy I spent propping up
an image of myself, trying to ensure that I got exactly what I

wanted or preserved what I had. Despite all the internal work I'd done, I was still stuck in my habitual patterns. There were days that sadness overtook me and I found it difficult not to attack or judge my many shortcomings, wishing I were different.

As I continued to observe myself and the surroundings, I noticed something else. There was danger in the air. I shared my apprehension with Zina.

"Pay attention to your intuition," she said. "By now you know the difference between your own stuff and whatever you might be sensing energetically. You're pretty good at reading energy."

"I can't make it out," I said. "It's like static on the radio. But I know something's not right."

"Keep an eye on it," she said. "Let me know what develops. In the meantime, stay focused on your practice."

By the third week my mindfulness practice had greatly improved, but the sense of danger had become almost tangible. I had a nagging feeling that I should leave Samadhi, but was afraid to venture away from this new cocoon I'd created. I decided to walk two hours to the nearest phone to call Sanda, hoping she could help me figure out the next step.

The tiny village of Hone Creek comprised a dirt road, a few small huts, and a little store with one public phone. I learned that I needed to buy a phone card, but the person who sold them was out to lunch. I sat outside the store beside a few stray dogs and their drunken owners, impatient and trying to rest with my breath. When the clerk finally returned, I bought a card and nervously dialed Sanda's number. I listened as the phone rang—once, twice, three times—and the dreaded machine came on.

"Hi, Sanda," I said. "It's Jess, from Costa Rica. I'm doing

okay—no actually, I'm not. This is much harder than I imagined and sometimes I can't remember why I came. I sense danger, but I don't know what it's about. I guess I'll try you another time. Hope you're well." I hung up.

I walked away feeling even more lonely and homesick. I was frustrated at the prospect of calling Sanda again and reaching her machine, but then I remembered something she'd said before I left: if we needed to connect, we would. If not, there was a lesson I needed to learn on my own.

I felt suddenly encouraged. Whatever trouble I was having, whatever danger I was sensing, it must be something I was capable of handling.

Chapter 3

TESTS

There is rain and then there is *rain*. All the structures at Samadhi had tin roofs, so a downpour sounded like a hailstorm. The noise was deafening, but it seemed to lessen the voices in my head so I didn't mind. I awoke early on a rainy morning to find Zina standing in the doorway. None of the rooms had locks. I thought I must have been dreaming, but when I rubbed the sleep from my eyes and shook my head, she was still there.

"We have a problem."

"What is it?" I asked. All I wanted was to roll over and go back to sleep.

"Our safe was stolen last night—everything's gone."

"What?" I bolted upright. My traveler's checks, passport, and return ticket were in that safe.

"I'll need a detailed list of your possessions," Zina was saying. "And the numbers on the checks if you have them."

At first I couldn't comprehend what was happening. But this was a real robbery and my things were really missing.

"We'll discuss it more at breakfast," she said, eyeing me closely. My expression must have conveyed my disbelief. Zina softened slightly, "Remember, Jessica, it's only stuff. Use this as an opportunity to reinforce what you've learned."

I sat there, incredulous. I thought about the American Express commercials where beautiful couples rode horseback along the beach just hours after losing all their money. I knew it couldn't be that easy—nothing ever was—and without a phone I wondered how I'd deal with the situation. All the cash I had was now in someone else's possession. What did this mean? Would I have to cut my trip short? Would I need to borrow money from my folks or clean toilets at Samadhi? My initial response was to freak out and assume the worst, or conversely, to remain in denial. But there was also something infinitely more interesting and subtle happening: part of me knew that regardless of the outcome, I'd be okay. This was the same part that knew I needed to leave Los Angeles and come here. This knowing presence was also the observer in my meditation, the dreamer in my sleep, and the intuitive that had been sensing danger. And while I wanted to trust this clarity of mind, it also frightened me. How might life be different if my thoughts and actions were no longer governed by the old conditioned fears?

By breakfast, everyone had gathered in the dining room, filling out paperwork distributed by the local police. The smell of coffee and freshly baked bread diluted the tension as the staff explained what had happened in a variety of languages—English, French, Italian, German. I was surprised that everyone seemed relatively calm.

One of the owners informed us that the robbery had been

an inside job. The retreat center hoped to recover our belongings, but assured us they would provide transportation into San Jose if our possessions were not found in a timely manner. We would just have to wait and see. I kept trying to perceive this as an opportunity to strengthen my practice, but it was a stretch, and my desire to leave increased.

During this time I made friends with George and Susan, a middle-aged couple from North Carolina. They were relaxed and easy to be with, and I enjoyed hearing about their years in Poona, India, studying under the enlightened master, Osho.

"What's it like to sit with an enlightened being?" I asked.

George's smile indicated the experience was remarkable. "It's hard to put into words," he said. "You just know you're sitting with someone who's awake, someone who's gone deeper and seen farther than the rest of us."

Maybe I should have gone to India instead, I thought. Perhaps I would have found enlightenment and held on to my passport. But was enlightenment something that could be found, or was it merely a signpost pointing toward what has never been lost? Intellectually I understood that awareness was ever-present, that I needn't go anywhere to find it. But I didn't really get it. If I had, I probably wouldn't have been in the jungle looking for it.

The next morning, when there was still no news about the robbery, the three of us decided to hike to one of the nearby waterfalls. It had rained heavily the night before, so the mud on the trail was thick and slippery, but the day was glorious. The sky was a brilliant cobalt blue. Tiny raindrops gathered among the trees, reflecting the morning sun. As we made our way along the path we spotted a sloth (imagine a cross between a panda and ET), slowly inching its way up a tree. Later we came upon a field of vultures, which made me hesitate. For a split second it felt like I was straddling two dimensions: the one I normally occupied, where I could see color and light and all the usual things, and one that seemed inexplicably dark. I looked back at my companions to see if they'd registered alarm, but they seemed unconcerned. Perhaps I was just imagining things.

I continued to lead the way, comfortable with the trail I had previously ventured down. George took special care watching out for his wife, lending a hand whenever necessary and going before her to make sure that the footing was safe. When we got to the steepest section of the hike, we scavenged around for walking sticks to use as leverage on the sharp downgrade. I looked out over the ridge and scanned the vast terrain; the rainforest seemed never-ending. I was always nervous when it came to this part of the hike, like I was knowingly and foolishly putting myself in danger to make it down that stupid ravine, forcing myself to pass some imaginary test.

As we approached the cliff side I felt a slight tug at my right foot. I remembered double-knotting my boots, but when I looked down, the laces had come undone. That's odd, I thought. These laces hadn't come undone before. And what was that tug? Maybe I was just inventing a reason not to climb down the mountain, but truthfully something didn't feel right. I should have said something, anything, but instead I bent down to re-lace my shoe, while Susan ventured ahead of me and began the descent.

George and I watched as the earth began to give way, tiny fissures hollowing into gaping holes as the side of the cliff collapsed, taking Susan with it. We watched as she tumbled and fell almost fifty feet below us. Then she lay there, unmoving. How could this be happening? We were just on a routine hike, enjoying the day. I looked to George and saw the terror in his eyes. I wanted to undo that moment or grow wings so I could fly down and save her. But I could do neither. Finally, Susan moved and looked up at us. We exhaled. Thank God she was alive.

George held vigil for his wife throughout the night in a local hospital, and early the next morning she went in for surgery. I later learned that the doctors were able to repair her leg, which had been broken in seven places.

My fantasy of going on a magical journey where everything was divinely guided was rapidly deteriorating. But why so many dark elements? Was I being tested? And if so, was the answer to continue dodging bullets, or to remove myself from the line of fire?

Two days later our possessions were found, buried deep in the jungle, curiously stowed and protected from the rain by a plastic Hefty bag. Except for the local currency, everything was returned to its rightful owner. It was as if the robbery never occurred. Even though everything appeared fine, I wanted to leave Samadhi before anything else happened. I told Zina I'd be departing the following morning.

I decided to spend my last day at the beach and meet with Zina later that afternoon to have her read my astrology chart, since she was a renowned expert. I'd always been fascinated by the notion that our past and present could be read celestially, that the course of our lives might somehow be predestined. Zina and I had arranged sessions before, but each time something had interfered. "Today," she assured me, "we will meet without fail."

When the driver dropped me off at the beach, we agreed on a time and place for pickup. I spent most of the day swimming in the turquoise water of the Caribbean, reflecting on the first month of my journey. By all estimation it was time to move on. At the appointed hour I showed up at the designated pickup point, but the driver wasn't there. I drank some water and found a patch of shade where I could watch the comings and goings of the tourists and the locals. Puerto Viejo attracted surfers from around the world, but for some reason, I didn't feel safe. Cabs were impossible to find, and I finally had to walk the five miles home. The road was long, the sun heavy.

As I approached the entrance to the property, I came upon three young boys on their way to go fishing. I smiled breathlessly and they smiled back. "Mucho cansado," I said, and rolled my eyes to indicate that I was pooped. They giggled. I loved the simplicity of that moment. The boys offered to take me along and we joked about what we might catch and who would do the cooking, but I was in no shape to do anything but lie down.

The next moment, we all came to an abrupt stop. There, on the side of the dirt road, was a small white Nissan that had plummeted headfirst into a ten-foot ditch. The shattered windshield and crushed front end told us that the driver had to be dead or hurt badly. My stomach knotted at the sight. Taking a breath, I exchanged a wave with the boys and walked past the gate into Samadhi. The moment I entered the compound, I knew there was trouble.

Rex, one of the owners, was driving away in a vehicle with several of his workers, heading up the mountain. I yelled for him to wait, but when I hopped in the truck I could sense concern. Rex informed me in a monotone that Zina had decided to come fetch me at the beach, but she never made it. Evidently she had blacked out while driving down the hill and lost control of the little white rental car.

"Didn't you see it?" he asked.

"Yes," I said. We rode the rest of the way in silence.

Why was Zina coming to get me? I wondered. What happened? Would she live? I'd heard that she'd suffered a blackout the previous week and I wondered if she had a serious illness. But something told me to keep quiet, so I did.

Later that afternoon, when things had settled down a little, I found out the accident was serious. Zina had gone through the windshield, broken several ribs, and crushed her sternum on the steering wheel. She was being monitored in a nearby hospital.

I wouldn't see Zina again, though later I heard she did make a full recovery.

The next morning I collected my stuff, and Rex drove me down the hill to catch the local bus. He kept his head down and didn't say a word the whole way. I knew he and Zina had been lovers for many years. As I got out of the truck, Rex leaned over quietly and said: "Zina asked me to deliver a message."

"What is it?" I asked.

"She said to tell you she's using what happened to strengthen her practice, and that you should do the same."

"I will," I said. "Please tell her I send my prayers."

Rex nodded, and I made my way down the dirt road to catch the next bus.

HACIENDA DEL SOL

There is no guide, no teacher, no authority.
There is only you — your relationship with others and
with the world — there is nothing else.

— *Krishnamurti*

Chapter 4

WATCHING FOR SIGNS

The only seat available was next to a drunk, who would elbow me every few minutes to share his latest revelation or point out some scenic spot. It was incredibly humid, and the only fresh air on the bus trickled through little rectangular slits near the ceiling. The close quarters together with the stale smell of alcohol made me so dizzy that to keep from passing out I climbed up on the seat and stuck my nose out the opening like a dog. When it started to rain, everyone glared, including my not-so-sober seat mate, but I stood my ground, stuffing as much of my face as possible into that little hole, sucking up the sweet mountain air, wondering where to go next. One thing was clear: I could not think my way to the other side.

What I needed to do was strengthen my ability to trust. Trust that while there wasn't enough oxygen on the bus, that while I'd had a bumpy start and things weren't exactly going as planned, my decision to come here would ultimately be worthwhile, not because I was running away from anything, but because I was running toward something that I could not yet see, almost like a gravitational pull.

I recalled a conversation I'd had with Sanda prior to my departure. "What if I get stuck?" I'd asked. "How will I know where to go or what to do?"

Sanda assured me that this was precisely the point. "An initiation of this sort will force you to strengthen your perceptive abilities beyond your present comprehension. You'll need to sense more than think, and trust more than force things to happen. Stay alert to the signs."

The only sign I could decipher had come a week earlier, before I'd left Samadhi, when a screenwriter from Los Angeles told me about a retreat center on the other side of Costa Rica called Hacienda Del Sol. She didn't know its location, nor did she have the phone number, but she suggested I call her when she returned to the States, maybe she could find the information. In the meantime, I was on my own. So, as the countryside whizzed by through sheets of rain, I opened up my map, hoping that some location would speak to me. I'd heard about many noteworthy spots—the mountains of Guanacaste, the volcano at Arenal, the gulf at Puntarenas, the national park at Manuel Antonio—but the place I gravitated to was Tamarindo. I liked the way it rolled off my tongue in a little dance. It sounded playful, hopeful.

Located at the tip of the Nicoya Peninusula, a roughly thumb-shaped protrusion comprising the southwestern section of Guanacaste, and separated from the mainland by the Golfo de Nicoya, Tamarindo is a lively beach community bustling with developmental fever: condo projects, mini-strip malls and several upscale resorts. Stepping off the bus I felt disoriented and unbelievably hot (the Nicoya Peninsula and much of Guanacaste constitute the country's hottest and driest region). I'd thought that the change in climate would be a good thing, to dry me out from the perpetual dankness of the rainforest. Now I realized that my body wasn't prepared for the oppressive temperatures.

At one o'clock in the afternoon, without much food or water and having been up for two days straight, I walked aimlessly down a dirt road in 110-degree desert heat in search of a place to sleep. I had to use every ounce of strength not to collapse into a puddle of tears by the roadside. Why was this so difficult? Why couldn't I check into a nice hotel, take a shower, use the telephone, eat a good meal, sleep, and then start my search? I had enough money, so why not? Because, I reasoned, as cars and motorbikes kicked up clouds of red dust, I was on a quest, which meant I had to endure hunger, fatigue, and my overall desire to give up and go home. But why did I feel the success of my endeavor had anything to do with where I stayed or what I ate or whether I hired a taxi? Why did I buy into the notion that in order to become more self-aware, I first had to abolish the self? I decided to catch a cab.

Just then, a large green and yellow bird with long blue feathers sprouting from its head landed about three feet away from me. It had an authoritative presence. It intimidated me a little, and I wanted to walk away from it, but stood there a minute to see what happened. Although I'd watched endless species of unfamiliar birds soaring through the skies at Samadhi, I hadn't seen one of these. Then the bird cocked his head, looked me straight in the eye, and began to talk.

As a little girl, I had thought I could communicate telepathically with animals. Now, even though my logical mind wanted to negate it, I attempted to converse with this bird; I felt certain that it had a message. I needed it to have a message. As I strained to hear it, the bird hopped over to me and jumped onto my foot. It glanced up at me once and began pecking my shoe, gently at first and then more aggressively.

Partly out of sheer exhaustion, partly out of disbelief, I stood there watching this bird go to town on my shoe, amused and surprised at its aggression, trying to stay alert in the face of my fatigue. Where was this bird from? I looked up and down the street—it was empty but for several skeleton trees and a few stray pigs. And where was everybody? Why was I standing in the road with a large bird attached to my foot like some lone scarecrow? I attempted to shake it off, worried that if I reached down it would attack my arm. Instead of letting go, it clung to my laces, refusing to release its grip. I looked down, exasperated; it looked up expectantly and continued on in the same manner. "Okay, I give. What do you want? What are you doing? That is enough!" But the bird wouldn't budge. And so, I walked, it clung, and on we went like this for some time. Was it planning to become my pet?

I started to think the whole thing was hilarious, until its sharp pecking began to hurt and I brusquely shook it off. The bird flew onto the branch of a nearby tree and watched me. Relieved, I sat down to take a sip of water and collect myself. It was hard to stay present; my impulse was to get up and resume my wandering, but something told me to stay put. I honestly felt this bird was trying to communicate, trying to make something known, but I couldn't figure out what, so we remained there, the bird in its tree, I on the ground, the intense sun overhead.

Then a word I'd never heard before popped into my mind: nosara. What is nosara? I wondered. I peered at the bird. Something told me to open up my map to search for the word. I didn't know how to spell it or even if it was a real place, but after combing the interior of Costa Rica, I discovered a tiny speck in the Nicoya Peninsula. Nosara. What was there? I didn't know for sure, but I had a strong feeling that it might be the location of Hacienda Del Sol. At least that's what I was hoping.

I decided to try an experiment: I would go to Nosara and see what happened. I didn't want to look back and think, if only I'd listened to that talking bird. Sanda was right, these odd experiences helped to refine and expand my perceptive abilities. But could I remain open and receptive under normal circumstances? Would I, in my ordinarily busy life, take time to notice, let alone converse with, a bird?

Two days and one agonizingly long hot bus ride later, I arrived by taxi at Hacienda Del Sol. Tucked away off a dirt road and several miles in from the beach, the Hacienda was indiscernible but for the little wooden sign with a yellow painted sun hanging on a post near the entrance. The driver honked at the front gate, and I peered out the window to see several small bungalows with thatched roofs standing in a row, with a larger rancho sitting farther up the hill. Centrally located in the middle of nowhere, the place looked deserted. Exhausted, I peeled the back of my legs from the brown vinyl seat covers and took a swig of water. Suddenly I wasn't sure I wanted to be here. I'd expended a lot of energy just trying to find the place, asking strangers in restaurants and hotels and on the street if they'd heard of the Hacienda, feeling like an annoying detective in my own mystery show, but I still had doubts. The truth was, while I was committed to following through with the experiment, while I hoped and believed that some guiding force was directing this whole thing, I was also aware that I had set myself up to fail, that no matter what the Hacienda had in store, it couldn't possibly deliver what I wanted.

The flash of a woman running through the jungle caught my attention. I wasn't sure whether I'd seen her or not—maybe in my overly fatigued and dehydrated state I had hallucinated—but soon a real woman did appear and unhitched the fence, signaling for us to enter. The driver pulled up the dirt road, and the girl with short blond curls sauntered alongside the car, gesturing hello with her eyes, closing the gate behind us. There was a raw beauty about her, gracefulness in the way she moved.

I yanked my luggage from the trunk, irritated at how much shit I was still hauling around, how disheveled I felt, and asked about a room. The woman studied me curiously, as if trying to determine what business I might have at the Hacienda, but she didn't ask. Instead she adjusted her sarong over her breasts and led me through a maze of trees and foliage to a private cabana. Inside, a jar of fresh flowers sat on a small dresser and seashells lined the windows, which were makeshift pieces of screen running two-thirds the way up the sides of the hut. The top third was open to the elements. Out of the corner of my eye I caught a flurry of motion; a tiny swarm of wasps attended to their hive up in the thatched roof. Great, I thought, just what I need, to shack up in a beehive. I'm allergic to bees. I was already itching all over owing to the attack of bed mites the night before.

The woman, Chloë was her name, left me to settle in, and an hour later I sat down with Menlha, the owner of the Hacienda. Menlha almost looked like she was from another planet. Maybe it was the glazed look in her eyes, or the shock of silver hair sprouting from her head, or the fact that she moved very, very slowly. I don't know what made me feel she had seen more than her share of things. In a way she reminded me of Sanda, not her appearance, but her deep presence. I also picked up a strange overall vibe. I couldn't tell if it was the people or the place or something less tangible, but it made me uncomfortable. Menlha seemed to sense my unease. "Why don't you relax awhile, " she said. "Join us for dinner, see if you like the place."

I nodded, a nap would do me good.

When I awoke it was dark. My clothes clung to my body, my hair was wet with perspiration. It took me a few minutes to remember where I was. I reached my arm out from under the mosquito netting and flicked on the low-voltage light by my bed. A cricket leapt across the concrete floor. Where was the bathroom? I needed to rinse off. I dug a flashlight out from the bottom of my suitcase, gathered a few toiletries, and wandered up the path leading to the washroom. By now I was used to communal living, and after showering with a few familiar-looking insects and reptiles, I sat down to dinner with a friendly group of people. I learned that the group, ten massage students, had been together for two months and had three weeks left to complete their massage training with Menlha. There were also a few strays: a surfer, a Swedish man, and a ballerina. The environment appeared relaxed and supportive, no remnants of the darkness that pervaded Samadhi. Nevertheless, I felt skeptical. Also, I had a feeling of being observed.

As I drifted off to sleep to the sound of Chloë practicing the guitar in the cabana next to me, I vowed to leave early the next morning.

∞

At six A.M. a chime sounded outside my hut. It was Menlha, awakening the group for their six-thirty meditation. I opened my eyes and looked around the room. The space seemed softer, less foreign than the night before. Still, I was prepared to leave, but when I heard the rustling of the wind through the palm fronds and caught sight of the glorious blue sky, I reconsidered. Maybe I'd stay a few days after all. It wasn't as if I had anywhere to be.

I spent the afternoon washing clothes and hiking around the property, trying to get oriented. The heat was stifling. Each move consumed precious energy and by nine o'clock that night I was worn out. I collapsed into the hammock outside my cabana and gazed upward. Rarely had I seen a sky so black or stars so bright. The galaxy pulsed with life. My blood seemed to pump in time with the cosmos and for a moment I experienced how everything was interconnected, all boundaries artificial. Tears welled as I buried my head in my hands, deeply moved.

Then a flicker of light caught my attention. My eyes followed the light as it moved across the ravine outside my hut and hovered over a shrub, pulsing like a heartbeat. For a long moment, I stared at the unmoving light. Suddenly, it started bouncing around the bush at lightning speed, then stopped. Time seemed to stand still, my eyes riveted on the pulsing light. Somehow it appeared to be tracking me, too. I watched for a long time, but eventually had to go to the bathroom. I apologized to the light and peed right there on the earth. The light didn't move.

An hour later, I was in bed in the hut, my thoughts focused on the strange ball of light. Part of me wanted to stay up and see what would happen, but I knew I could bear only so much before slipping into denial or shutting down. The mind's ability to compartmentalize is a built-in protection mechanism, and already I had minimized what had happened, trying to figure out what else the light could be—an animal, a flashlight, the reflection of the moon—anything that would explain why a ball of light might be prancing around the forest. I reasoned that if I went inside and fell asleep, maybe it would just go away. Though I'd fantasized about an extraordinary event like this happening, something that would arrest my rationality and force me to see things differently, when actually faced with a mystery, my inclination was to get rid of it.

I stared at the shifting ceiling shadows until sleep came. At four A.M. I opened my eyes. The room was filled with platinum light. Slowly, I sat up. A white, glowing ball hovered at the foot of my bed.

"My God. What are you? What do you want?" I yelled.

The light retracted through the screen door, leaving me alone in the darkness. I wrapped my arms around my chest. What the hell was going on? White lights hovering in my room. Was I losing my mind?

For a long while, I stared at the screen door, expecting the light to return, but it never did.

Chapter 5

CROSSING OVER

After meditation I pulled Menlha aside to share what had happened. She listened quietly while I spoke. I assumed she thought I was a bit whacked, but she gave me her full attention. When I finished, she just nodded. "The locals say we're located over some sort of power center, an opening in the earth," she said. "There've been reports of flying saucers and other strange things. I've been watching what I think is a UFO come in and out over that hill"—she pointed west. "Maybe you had a visitor last night."

All I could do was look into her eyes, searching. It wasn't exactly that I didn't believe her, at this point I was pretty much open to anything, but it was not a conversation I'd ever had before, talking about UFOs and extraterrestrials. Part of me was riveted, the other part just plain stunned.

She nodded again. "Yeah, the saucers have been around a lot lately. In fact Chloë sees them come through around two A.M. You might want to ask her about them."

Menlha went on to explain the history of the land and how

an ancient Indian civilization had once occupied this territory. When she first bought the land about four years earlier, she said the spirits were raging and the energy was very dark. She brought in a shaman to perform ceremonies to cleanse the land and release energies that had been imbedded here for centuries. Only in the past year had things quieted down. I began to put the pieces together, better able to understand my general uneasiness. This place was loaded with invisible energies.

At breakfast, I asked about what others had seen while living at the Hacienda. Several people in the group talked about different sightings, including a little ghost boy that hung out on the mountain peak, and electric colors that lit up the night sky. To some it seemed normal. Others were skeptical, though these occurrences were supposedly a common thing at the Hacienda. Menlha suggested that maybe I'd been led here for a reason. But what reason could that be? To track white lights and communicate with extraterrestrials? The prospect made me laugh out loud. But reality as I knew it was expanding, I couldn't argue with that.

In addition to being attractive to aliens, the earth under the Hacienda was rich in texture and nutrients, and people came from all around to bathe in the mud. That afternoon, Chloë and I collected some muddy earth and headed to the San Juanillo cove. We'd sort of become instant friends. I kept trying to figure out why I was so drawn to Chloë, so captivated. She was beautiful, but it wasn't that; it was something richer, more soulful.

As we walked along the path to the beach, I had the distinct sense that we'd been swept up into a current of energy, as if we were leaving one dimension and entering another. Colors went from bright to brighter, sensations increased and thoughts diminished. I hushed the periodic voices in my head that told me I was just imagining things. I wasn't. I let my imagination roll: what would it be like to travel to another place in time?

The sheltered bay was calm and the water glistened a transparent aquamarine. The sand was coarse, composed of tiny shells in many colors. Remnants of a shipwreck were strewn along the beach. That was weird, so weird that it almost didn't register as being real, more like a backdrop put there for effect. In fact the whole area had a surreal quality, including the Hacienda, as if this sliver of the planet had been preserved in its natural state of wonder and mystery.

Chloë and I peeled away our clothing and dove into the ocean. After a short swim we got busy with the mud, applying layer upon layer, until only our eyes and hair were visible. Once baked, we scurried over to the tide pools and, like seals, slipped in and out of the water until we were clean. I took a long nap and dreamed of vultures and dry barren land. Lying next to me was Chloë, suddenly seeming like the goddess, the one who gives life. I was enchanted with her. I began to wonder if my growing infatuation was a way for me to connect with this lost part of myself.

Later that afternoon I found a note from her slipped under my door, thanking me for the day. The letter was written on a hand-painted card, the envelope sealed with a postage stamp from Antigua, Guatemala. Three tiny words were written underneath the stamp: YOU MUST GO. Chills ran down my spine. What was in Guatemala and why would Chloë tell me to go there? I made a mental note to ask her about it later.

That night, Chloë and I huddled up in my hammock, scouting for white lights. She told me that she'd died on the operating table from cardiac arrest at age twenty. Said she saw images, apparitions. She described the encounter as the most peaceful moment of her life, and though she came back to reenter her body, she never forgot it. While she was talking I spotted the white light, only this time it was much closer, maybe ten feet away. "There it is," I whispered.

Chloë looked in the direction I had pointed, but as she did, the light disappeared. Figures. But soon the light returned and Chloë saw it too. She didn't seem surprised. "It looks like a curious one tonight," she said.

We sat for a while, watching. As time passed I became more comfortable, until gazing at the light felt almost normal. Almost. I guess I had become desensitized. Eventually, we both grew sleepy and decided to call it a night. Spent, I fell asleep in my hammock and had a vision:

A powerful wind blows through the ravine and the colors are electric red, green, and yellow. Many lights exit a saucer, but only one comes toward me as I sit waiting. Without realizing what's happening, I feel the light enter my body followed by an explosion of inconceivable pleasure. I am tingling and vibrating—I want it to last forever. As I bask in this ecstasy I hear a message: God is the energetic frequency of love. You must know this, live this, and share this. That is all.

I awoke the next morning feeling as if I had ventured far away and needed to stuff my soul back into its frame. Was the UFO moment a dream, or did it really happen? And what was the difference? Either way, my psyche was busy digesting it all. At breakfast Chloë looked across the table and asked, "Did you see the saucer come through last night? The colors were brilliant."

I nodded and looked around to see if anyone was listening, before I told her about the vision. "What am I supposed to do with white lights and flying saucers and information about God?"

"Nothing," she assured me. "You crossed over into another dimension, had an experience with another life form, but the same laws apply. Maybe it'll return, maybe it won't. Try not to attach too much meaning or fall prey to the illusion that it's going to change your life. It's like when I had my vision on the operating table. The images were beautiful to see and they increased my faith, but it didn't solve my problems in this life."

I knew she was right, but secretly I hoped that the light would return, that I might receive another message. Somehow one wasn't enough.

Nearly two weeks passed at the Hacienda with no sign of the light or the saucer, and I began to get nervous. Was the UFO vision supposed to be the grand finale? And if so, why didn't I feel any different? I was still clinging to the belief that if I had the right experience or revelation, I'd be instantly transformed, self-realized. And yet, I was aware that this was a little game I was playing, a fantasy, because it was easier to focus on channeling information than to face my own confusion. It was easier to believe that someone or something else had the power to change my life, than to stare directly into my frustrating solitude. The group was nearly finished with their training and Menlha would be closing up shop. I would be forced to move on, again.

Central America was preparing for the rainy season. As the humidity increased, the heat rose and the air became thick and still. Offering the promise of rain and cool relief, the clouds hovered, but were not swollen enough yet to help us. Everyone moved slower, vacantly staring off into space, and we all were sweating, even in the dead of night. We knew there was nothing to do but wait.

The intense heat triggered my headaches. I lay in my hammock barely clothed, a cold washcloth draped over my eyes, while Chloë gave me cranial massages to help ease the pressure. I knew that my time in Costa Rica was coming to a close, I could feel it, but I wasn't ready to head home. I hadn't gotten what I needed. My brain, however, refused to work in any kind of order and at times I felt close to delirium. I wanted to talk to Sanda, get some direction and reassurance, but I was too weak to walk the few miles into town to use the phone.

Several days passed before I regained my strength. I headed to the bluff to watch the sunset and pray for rain. The cloud formations began to take on a life of their own; I saw strange shapes and images as I moved about the dry brush. Even the normally robust pochote trees looked more like bare mangled limbs than anything resembling flora. An anteater scampered up ahead, no doubt in search of water. The terrain was bleak, and I was relieved when Chloë emerged out of the shrub. "What's gotten into you?" she asked. "You look terrible."

I smiled wearily. "Just confused."

"You worry too much," she said. "This doesn't have to be so difficult. Let go of your expectations and your plans, just be open to what comes. Let your journey unfold."

"I am open." My words sounded forced.

"Be patient," Chloë said. "The answer will come, it always does."

Chloë and I scanned the horizon. There was nothing and nobody as far as the eye could see, except the storm. We watched it move in, anticipating the cool relief. The gentle breeze caressed our skin, giving us a sweet taste of what was to come.

Then came the first big rain of the season. With it came the army ants. Costa Rica is known for them. They clean out everything in their path. Legend has it that if army ants are milling about your room when you go to bed, it is better not to sleep there, just in case. Clearly, it was time to move on.

Chapter 6

ZEN SURFING

My last night at the Hacienda was difficult. Everyone in the group had a plan, returning home to family, work, the responsibilities of life. I was at a loss. I cleaned my room and packed up my things, all the while praying for some direction. I sat on the bed and forced myself to take a deep breath. Thoughts swirled around my brain—Where are you going? What's going to happen? You'll never figure this out—and I felt helpless to stop them. I collected my books and note pads, carefully tucking them away into my bag, doubting myself.

Chloë's letter fell out. I remembered our day on the beach and smiled. I glanced at the envelope, the postage stamp from Guatemala, and her scrawled words, YOU MUST GO. Again I got the chills. I had no idea what was in Guatemala, nor did I want to travel to another country, but I was desperate and needed a plan. And on some level I felt it was a sign, just like the talking bird, a moment when things came inexplicably together to help move me along. But I had a tough time trusting that life could be that simple.

At dinner I got into a conversation with Francisco, the surfer who'd managed to remain mostly invisible throughout my three-week stay. Francisco was an olive-skinned Salvadorian, his long, flat nose resembling the Indian-head profile on the face of the nickel. Francisco told me he'd grown up in Los Angeles, after he and his mother had fled their homeland. He became a lawyer and tried to live a conventional life, but he said something was always missing. Eventually he made his way back to Central America and settled in Costa Rica, mostly to surf, but he maintained a real estate business on the side. He mentioned that he was heading to the Osa Peninsula, to visit a friend and do some surfing. Did I want to come along? I was thrown by his offer. After all, the plan was to go to Guatemala. Yet, I felt a pull to go with him.

"Sounds fun," I said. "But I'm sort of traveling alone these days."

"Okay," he said. "Just thought you might enjoy the Osa—it's a great spot."

It would be nice to take a break, I thought, but was he interested in getting involved romantically? I'd heard that he'd been involved with two of the massage students at the Hacienda. Until now, most of the Latin men I'd met seemed to have one thing on their minds, and I just wasn't interested.

"Friends?" I asked.

He laughed. "If a friend is what you're looking for, then friends it is."

"Great," I said. "Let's do it." Guatemala would have to wait.

∞

Located at the southernmost tip of the country, the Osa Peninsula is one of the most remote places in Costa Rica. Surrounded by thick jungle and ocean, the area is known for its rich wildlife and world-class waves. We flew into Puerto Jimenez and headed to the local market to load up on food for the week. Our taxi, a pickup truck with room for us to stand in the back, took off into the jungle. Although it was the rainy season, we were graced with gorgeous weather. We bounced along on the dirt road, periodically sneaking a peek at the rugged coastline, applying bug repellent to guard against the mosquitoes.

The house was situated about fifty meters from the sea, right on Backwash Bay, one of the best surf spots in Costa Rica. The structure was completely open, at once primitive and luxurious. A gourmet kitchen and Balinese-style showers were set outside and everything was propane and solar powered. The ocean was visible from all sides and there were no doors, no locks, no mirrors, and no clocks. Only the jungle and the sea. We unloaded our groceries and headed straight to the beach.

Francisco told me that this bay was often calm, but throughout my stay I would not see it calm enough for swimming. In fact, we had arrived during one of the season's biggest swells. Being from California I was used to being near the ocean and surfers, but the waves in Matapalo were breaking at a monstrous twenty feet. Francisco surfed every day, and even managed to get me in the water on three separate occasions that week: once for swimming, once for kayaking, and once for surfing. Each time I was sure I was going to die.

For meals we cooked up the local fare: black bean soup, ceviche, tamales, plantains, and we picked mangos and papayas right off the trees. We read aloud, hiked, napped, and competed in a serious gin rummy tournament. We danced without music, sang a cappella at the top of our lungs, and sat up late each night contemplating the universe. I slept deeply and peacefully, yet I still had doubts about what I was doing. I didn't want to lose sight of my original intention, which, while somewhat vague, did not include getting distracted by a man. That much I knew.

Toward the end of the week, Francisco urged me into the water to practice surfing at a nearby beach where the waves were more manageable. I'd never been much of a surfer. I'd tried it a few times but I couldn't relax enough to enjoy it. I liked hanging out in the shallow water and frolicking along the beach, but was basically afraid of the waves and the world beneath the sea, especially sharks. I was counting on Francisco to be my guide.

I felt awkward on the long board, trying to figure out which movements were necessary and which were counterproductive. Paddling out, I dodged and submerged myself on cue. A colossal wave approached and I inhaled a gulp of air before going under, hoping to drop deep enough to miss the blow. But I got caught. The wave set me tumbling downward with a force so strong it was useless to struggle. I clung to the leash, the plastic strap attaching my ankle to the surfboard, to keep from panicking.

When I resurfaced, the ocean had gone mysteriously flat, no hint of the force we had just negotiated. I struggled to catch my breath and remount the board. Gazing around, I took a moment to admire the landscape, the unrestrained rainforest, and the late-afternoon sun slipping behind silver clouds. It was almost peaceful, until a sharp prickling sensation ran down my leg and my right knee went numb. Francisco only laughed when he saw the terror in my eyes; I'd been stung by a jellyfish.

"No worries," he said. "The numbness will disappear in a few minutes." But while I waited I was stung twice more.

Now I just wanted to get out of there, but Francisco encouraged me to relax, to enjoy the beauty, and to practice "that

meditation stuff," aptly pointing out that it was of little value
if I couldn't pull it up on demand. I was in the midst of a lesson
in the art of Zen surfing.

A local Tico boy was surfing near us, his lean body sculptured
by endless hours of paddling. He smiled a friendly hello, but I
felt too miserable and swamped by my own anxiety to respond.
I was isolated and way out of my league. I looked out to sea and
tried to focus on the sheet of tranquil turquoise water. Farther
out a dolphin was playing, unaffected by the surf, and a peli-
can flew by, expertly skimming the surface. It was silent in the
ocean. All was harmonious, all except me.

Abruptly, Francisco yelled for me to start paddling toward
shore. He was immediately by my side, giving me a small shove,
and before I could argue he had me positioned to catch the next
wave. The Tico boy had already caught it and I watched him
descend from above, riding the tube with easy confidence.

Francisco shouted instructions: "Steady your board, find
your balance, stay calm."

I responded to his cues, my hands pressed into the waxy surface of the board and, as in yoga, I used my abdomen to lift
my body and scoot my feet under my hands, wobbling slightly.
I spotted a fish surfing next to me, its long body visible in the
transparency of the swell. Somehow this inspired me, gave me
the extra push to stand up, to trust that I could do it. And I
did—for a few precious seconds I actually stood up and surfed
alongside this wide-eyed fish. Then of course I lost my balance
and fell backwards.

When it was nearly dark and we were cold and hungry, we
began our slow return. A medium set rolled in and I found
myself caught between two waves, taking Francisco's advice
to ride in lying flat on my board. Coming in was always scary,
unpredictable, as I was totally at the mercy of the tide. I felt

my stomach drop, my heart pounding furiously against the board. Will I or won't I make it in safely? But when I reached the crest of the wave, I saw that it was going to break right on the sand. I was going down and there was no water underneath to cushion my fall.

My chin collided with the hard surface; sharp pains ricocheted through my back as the board attempted to yank me back out to sea. Submerged in a whirling black blur, I felt the coarse sand and rocks scrape me. I didn't have the energy to panic, so I waited, hoping the current would release me. I remembered that my mother, as a young child, had nearly drowned in the ocean, and I wondered if this was how I was going to die. That's when everything went dark.

Coming to, I found myself beached on the incline, a few feet from the ten-foot waves hammering the shore. I knew I was alive and immediately tried to crawl to safe territory, only to find my body was deadweight. With the little strength I had, I glanced back to see how much time I had before the next wave would come in. Mercifully, Francisco arrived along with it, but his face and his silence told me that I looked ravaged. He demanded that I get up. I teetered until I found my balance. Pain shot through me.

It was dark and cold, we had no towels or shoes, and our place was a mile's walk on the muddy dirt road. Rain threatened. I took a deep breath to muster the strength to walk and felt myself enter a light trance. With my teeth chattering and my skin covered in sand, I stubbed my toes constantly as we stumbled through the darkness, thinking if there were ever a good time to practice detachment from the physical body, this was it. A swarm of biting flies, hungry for the salt on our skin, appeared out of nowhere and covered my bikini-clad body. I felt their tiny assaults, knowing they were drawing blood. I would have collapsed to the ground if I'd allowed myself to think about what was happening. If I stopped moving, the flies would happily eat me alive. If I opened my mouth to speak, I would have flies for dinner. I thought about the house. The clouds moved in and the wind picked up; it would be pouring in minutes. Still, I focused all my energy on visualizing the house, and when we rounded the next bend, there it was.

I dreaded getting into the cold shower, but there was no hot water and I had to rinse off the sand and the flies. The rain poured down outside the open stall as I hurried through the process of rinsing, soaping, and drying off. Light-headed and freezing cold, I placed my attention on my breath—inhaling to the count of eight and exhaling to the count of eight—reaching into the bedrock of yoga. I continued to breathe until I was dressed and wrapped up in bed.

Then I collapsed.

I am flying through a tunnel or some kind of cave. I pass several lions and jaguars as I head toward the distant fire. Have I died? If so, where are the white lights? I don't think fire is a good sign.

Finally, I reach my destination, hovering above the flames, where I see a peaceful-looking man wearing a red head wrap. His eyes are gentle. He invites me to look into the fire to see my destiny. I am so excited I can barely contain myself; finally someone is going to reveal my future. He smiles knowingly as I bow my head over the blaze and we wait. But I can't see anything, and I begin to get frustrated. The Buddha-like man touches my third eye, calming me. My life begins to scroll out before me.

I catch glimpses of different people and events—family gatherings, friends, people in different parts of the world, bombings, terror, trees, flowers, making love, fighting, starvation—watching as I pass through the different stages of life, much like what I imagine happens when a soul passes from life to death. Everything I have ever said or done is before me, whether it's a fight with my mother, a joke with a stranger, or inhaling a whiff of fresh-baked chocolate chip cookies. I see how I've treated myself and others. I see the suffering when I have withheld love and the joy when I have given it. I see that it is I who determine whether I live in heaven or hell by the choices I make each and every day. The universe is providing the lens, but I am the sole witness. There is no one else.

I awoke thirty-six hours later with a monster hangover. Francisco was asleep in the chair next to my bed, a bucket of cold water and washcloths at his feet. I was alive, but disoriented. My head was pounding and my body felt like a bag of brittle bones. I tried to get up, but my back went into spasm. I resigned myself to lie still and think. I needed to talk to Sanda.

I dialed her number on Francisco's cellular phone. Holding back a torrent of tears, I felt that I had ruined everything. Gratefully, she answered.

"Sanda, it's Jess. I think I'm in trouble."

"I could feel you've been struggling, what's going on?"

I told her what I could remember about the accident. While I had survived, I was afraid I wouldn't recover quickly enough to continue. How could I have made such a wrong turn? Sanda listened while I told her about my dream, the man with the head wrap and the gentle smile. I had a vivid sense that he was important but I didn't know what to do next.

"Have faith in your vision," Sanda said. "Sit patiently, meditate on your dream and see if you can get a sense. And trust yourself."

Her words helped.

Later that day, Francisco brought in a chiropractor to adjust my neck and back, which had been tweaked in the fall. At one point, when they thought I was asleep, I overheard Francisco relay the details of the accident. The doctor said I was lucky not to be returning home in a body bag. I cringed. It took me two weeks to recover. The chiropractor advised me to fly home instead of remaining in Central America, but now that wasn't an option.

During those two weeks, I couldn't stop thinking about the man with the red head cover. He looked indigenous, with dark skin and a round belly. I wondered about the symbolism of the fire and red cloth. I asked Francisco if there was a region in Central America where the men dressed like this, but he was at a loss. I'd always been curious about the Mayan culture, and the more I meditated, the more I pictured my visitor as a Mayan Indian. Suddenly, I felt I was back on the right track. In fact, I was certain that this man held a key. I was on my way to Guatemala to find him.

ANCIENT MAYA

There are only two ways to live your life.
One is as though nothing is a miracle.
The other is as though everything is a miracle.

— *Albert Einstein*

Chapter 7

EGG CEREMONIES

I arrived in Guatemala City, a diesel-fuming, horn-honking nightmare, with not the slightest clue how to locate the man from my dream. After passing through customs and a sea of semiautomatic rifles, I hailed a cab and headed toward the mountains, to a small city called Antigua, once the capital of Guatemala, where I would spend a few days to chart out my course. As the taxi curved through the lush mountain pass, I exhaled a long, deep sigh. I was weary. It was late morning and billowing white clouds traversed the blue sky. Towering volcanoes loomed in the distance.

Antigua is an old colonial village, with cobblestone streets and vine-covered ruins, permeated by the Mayan culture. Villagers line the main square selling tortillas, frijoles con arroz, pan dulce, and various crafts, including hand-woven textiles, glazed pottery, and ceremonial wooden carvings. A Mariachi band strolls through Central Park, creating a time-warp effect, proclaiming that all is well in the world, while a dozen military officers form a human blockade a few yards to the north, in front of the double-colonnaded Palacio del Ayuntamiento, Antigua's town hall. This was the same military responsible for an Indian massacre in the early 1980s, and the assassination of Bishop Girardi a year before my visit.

The country was volatile now. Guatemala was preparing for its first election since the peace accord. I'd heard personal accounts of tourists who'd been pulled off buses and forced to lie spread-eagled on the ground while their wallets were stolen, passports confiscated. Often they were beaten. But of course there were plenty of people who had pleasant experiences in Guatemala. I had only one reason to travel to such an unstable country: I was on a mission.

There were other risks as well, including my headaches, which had become considerably worse since the surfing mishap. Francisco had brought in a good doctor, but he didn't have much effect. I'd been dealing with the headaches for nearly ten years, and though at times the symptoms could be alleviated, the pain never went away completely, it lived just beneath the surface. I felt the familiar pressure starting to build: temples throbbed, vision blurred, my brain operated in slow motion. I was desperate for relief, and after a week of getting no closer to finding the man from my vision, I began to lose hope.

I wandered down an empty cobblestone street while rain fell. Dirty wet hair got plastered to my head. Lightning leapt across the surrounding mountains, and the sky exploded with thunder. Before long I was caught in a hailstorm. I ducked into the nearest storefront with a little video parlor in back and decided to catch a movie to pass the time. They were showing a National Geographic documentary called *Maya: The Lost Kingdom*, so I bought a ticket and ordered a cup of tea.

I had a few minutes before the film started, so I settled in to watch the people try to escape the rain. June is one of the rainiest months in Central America and I daydreamed about what the weather might be like in California. I was missing home. Soon, a young couple entered the store and bought tickets to the show. There was no place left to sit, so I offered to share my table. The two looked about my age, and I was especially drawn to the woman; I thought I detected something behind her eyes, something inquisitive. Or maybe I was just lonely and needing a friend. She spoke in Spanish, though she was American. Apparently, she'd once lived in Guatemala and had returned to give her fiancé the grand tour. I wondered if she could help me out.

"So, did you have any contact with the Indians when you lived here?" I asked, after we'd concluded our introductions.

"They keep to themselves mostly, unless they're trying to sell you something." She smiled.

"What about up in the highlands, away from the tourists?" I asked. "I'd like to spend some time, get to know the Mayan people."

The woman shifted in her chair. She had well-defined cheekbones, the tiny muscles in her jaw twitched in thought. "I did know a man up at the lake, Lago de Atitlán," she said. "But I'm not sure he's still there."

I'd been thrown a crumb, and it was just enough to keep me going. I think it was Confucius who said, "Perseverance furthers." I wasn't so sure. Sometimes I felt like I was just running in circles, accomplishing nothing. But as I watched the documentary, in which archeologists and excavation teams dedicated themselves to uncovering the ancient Mayan mysteries, often working years before hitting any concrete sign of progress, I gained perspective. I saw that my own intention was similar: to uncover the lost and forgotten aspects of myself so I could remember who I really was.

∾

L ago de Atitlán is an awesome sight, crouching at the feet
of three volcanoes at the southern end of the Guatemalan
highlands. The water is like an expansive sheet of jade, and the
surrounding mountains are blanketed by green velvet. Too bad
the lake is ridden with parasites—there's no proper sewage. It
runs ten miles across and nearly 1000 feet deep. The natives
refer to Atitlán as the navel of the world; they believe that this
is where everything started. In the morning, the jade-colored
water is as smooth as glass, but in the afternoon, the Xocomil,
a southeasterly wind, stirs up the liquid mysteries.

Laurette, the woman from the film, told me to catch the bus
from Antigua to Los Encuentros. "You'll find transportation
there that'll get you past Sololá to Panajachel, the first town by
the lake," she said. "It'll take about three hours, but the scenery's great.

"On your way, check out some of the small villages in the
highlands. The people's ways of life, their traditions and val-
ues, are quite strong in the region. That's probably why I gravitated there. Unfortunately, all the guerrilla activity has really
weathered the area."

I admired Laurette's confidence and knowledge of the area,
but I didn't have a lot of energy. "So what's this guy's name?"
I'd asked.

"There's a woman who sells jewelry in Panajachel," she told
me. "Her name's Cat. Tell her you're a friend of mine. If Joselo's up at the lake, she'll know where."

"Joselo." I said the name aloud so I'd remember.

"Good luck."

"Thanks." My head was killing me. But I savored the uncer-
tainty of that moment, the recognition that I was at a cross-

roads, the anticipation of tracking down some strange man, a Mayan Indian, and wondering if he might change the course of my trip. It was a subtle shifting of the lens, so that I was no longer just on a general quest; now my search had a very precise focus. This helped me to feel better, more secure; finally I had something concrete to go on. I had only one reservation. What exactly did I hope would happen once I found Joselo? Was I just setting myself up, driven to locate this man at the lake like Dorothy in search of Oz?

Like many of the small villages surrounding the lake, Panajachel (Pana for short) is composed of a few meandering streets and one main drag where the locals come to sell their goods. Nicknamed gringotenango, place of the foreigners, Pana seems to attract plenty of tourists and artists and layabouts. It's also relatively easy to get to, compared to other areas around the lake that are only accessible by boat.

I wandered into town and inquired about Cat, the jewelry lady. The vendors pointed me in every direction, and after a frustratingly long scavenger hunt I found her down by the water's edge, sitting quietly next to an array of amber and amethyst trinkets displayed on a purple velvet cloth. Cat was a hearty-looking woman, maybe twenty-five years old, with flushed cheeks and Pippy Longstocking braids. I said hello and told her about my meeting with Laurette, that I was looking for Joselo. After negotiating a fee for her to accompany me across the lake, Cat agreed to take me to Santiago Atitlán, a part of the lagoon squeezed between the towering volcanoes of Tolimán and San Pedro, to meet Joselo.

Crossing Atitlán is breathtaking. Magnificent volcanic peaks give way to rising waterfalls and colorful hillsides dotted with men and woman working the fields. I dangled my fingers overboard, trailing tiny wakes in the jade-colored water. It felt like

I had pierced a veil, stepped over a threshold. I glanced at Cat, her bronze cheeks glowing in the late-afternoon sun. She asked me what I needed, that I should seek out a shaman. I blinked. I hadn't been told that Joselo was a shaman, but of course it made perfect sense, as much sense as anything else did on this trip.

We arrived in Santiago with the rain. On rickety stilted docks sat women hunched over, washing clothes at the lakeshore. They looked up from their work and smiled. I wondered if they ever had the desire to go out seeking.

Cat and I climbed the rainy cobblestone streets of Santiago de Atitlán, in search of a shaman.

Joselo's house was typical of the Guatemalan style—rectangular with a tiny atrium in the center, tile floors throughout, a tin roof above. I entered what appeared to be a living room, or sala, though it looked more like an overcrowded art gallery, the walls teeming with abstract paintings of the Mayan women. I was fascinated by the intricate detail in the compositions, the patterns in the fabrics, and the candid expressions of the women. Cat motioned for me to have a seat. I melted into the well-worn velour couch, head spinning, body aching. What was I going to say to this man?

Fifteen minutes later, I was introduced to a short, bearded man with glasses and a very calm disposition. There was sort of a glow around him, although it could have been the fog from my headache. Anyway, he seemed to possess an inner stillness. I examined him more closely. It wasn't as though he looked the spitting image of the man in my dream; he didn't dress in white or wear a red head covering. In fact, he looked pretty ordinary, except for the sparkle in his eyes and his soothing presence, but

I had the distinct feeling that everything that had occurred over the past three months had been leading up to this moment, that each encounter had somehow contributed to my being here with this man.

He stared at me, never breaking eye contact, until eventually I got skittish. I felt completely exposed.

"Welcome," he said finally. "I have wait for you to come." His words were a mixture of Spanish and English. I guess he knew I wouldn't understand his native Quiché dialect.

I was caught off guard by the certainty in his voice. How could it be that this Mayan shaman who lived in the mountains of Guatemala was anticipating my arrival? He probably said this to everyone.

I wanted to say something—Who are you? How'd you know I was coming? But no words would come out. Joselo grinned. Maybe he was used to this sort of thing. "First I talk," he said. "After, you ask questions."

He unfolded a piece of paper filled with strange signs and symbols, they almost looked like hieroglyphics. "What's that?" I asked.

He smiled, reminding me that he was doing the talking and I was doing the listening.

"Oh, sorry," I said.

"I have prepare your Mayan horoscope," he said. "It tells of our meeting." He paused to sip some water. I was confused. Since when did he know my date of birth?

"You seek balance, no?" he asked.

It was sort of a vague question. I mean, who wasn't seeking balance? Everyone I knew was trying to balance work, friends, family, creativity, service, and life in general. But if Joselo was referring to the kind of balance necessary to live a normal life and feel truly rooted in oneself, to fully participate in the world and remain conscious while doing so, then yes, I suppose I was.

"Each of us must find our destiny," he continued, "or we will not be happy. For you, this means faithful commitment to spiritual life." I wondered what he thought I was doing in Central America, sitting in his living room, without a job.

"Are you writer?" he asked.

"No, not really."

"Yes, you are writer."

"Oh."

"But first you must develop wisdom," he went on. "You are powerful woman. You are Jun Q'anil, one who walks the way. You will come to know secrets of universe. Then you must use knowledge to help others. And one day," he added, "you will have disciples of your own."

When he asked about my health, I lied and said I was fine. I didn't know why I lied; maybe it was denial or wishful thinking or maybe the health issue seemed too complicated to get into, but somehow he knew. He knew that my health hadn't been good. He told me that my ovaries and reproductive area were vulnerable and as a result, I was not a good candidate for casual sex. In fact, "No sex at all for you," he said. "You must control animal desires, use energy to tap into higher realms. You must purify, get rid of toxic energy. Then you have happy and healthy life. If you no listen to your destiny, your health will continue poorly.

"The more you purify, the stronger you make intuition," he said. "Do not forget, you are here to make good the work of Spirit."

I didn't tell him about my headaches, but again, he seemed to know anyway. He inquired about the pressure in my head, how long I had suffered, what usually preceded the pain, and how I had sought relief in the past. I gave him a brief history

about my life, my health difficulties, my work, and my decision
to leave everything behind and come here. He listened to every
word. When I had finished talking he said, "Come tomorrow. I
perform egg ceremony. It help with blockage."

Before I could ask any further questions he said, "Mañana,
a las cuatro. Adios."

Even though the pressure in my head was verging on unbearable, there was a slight hop in my step and a lightness about me
because I had met this man, whoever he was.

By early afternoon the next day, I headed to the mercado, its
open stalls and narrow, winding corridors covering several
blocks. That day there was a power outage due to the heavy
rain, so the vendors lit candles, giving the scene a watery lumi-
nescence. I saw everything from fresh flowers to dead cows as I
moved swiftly through the porticos in search of the ingredients
I'd been instructed to bring to the ceremony: two white candles,
two eggs, and agua florída (purified flower water).

By coincidence, I had run into Joselo twice that morning,
on two separate occasions, on two different street corners.
The first time he appeared young and vibrant, the next limp-
ing and gaunt. It was odd, as if Joselo were two different people. I thought about what he had said when I bought the eggs:
"Egg is living organism. It take negative energy stored in body,
removes blockages, help energy to flow." I didn't trust the idea
that an egg could make my head stop hurting, but decided that
if I got even a bit of relief, I'd stay and see what I could learn
from this man.

At four o'clock I arrived at his house, excited and a little
nervous. I listened to the rain splatter against the tin roof and

smelled the aroma of unrecognizable herbs brewing on the big iron stove. Joselo led me down a dark hallway until we entered his ceremonial space, a small nook containing three tiny tables holding a smattering of candles, crystals, and several sacred Mayan artifacts. He motioned for me to sit facing the altar. He told me to focus my attention on two glasses of water. He put on some sort of head covering, but it wasn't red. Shadows danced against the adjoining wall and Joselo instructed me to concentrate on the pain in my head. That wasn't difficult.

He began the ritual by pouring agua florída over my entire body, necessary to protect my chakras, or energy centers, from unwanted invasion. He whispered an invocation, a mixture of Spanish and Quiché, as he took a raw egg still in its shell and began to rub it over me. My head, spinal area, solar plexus, and second chakra received the most attention, but he was thorough and the egg went everywhere. Strangely, I trusted Joselo, I felt so the moment I'd met him, but now that I was engaged in a formal ritual I questioned whether I'd acted too quickly. Maybe I should have asked for his credentials. But no, this was where I was supposed to be. At least that's what I told myself.

Joselo moved like an elf, working the egg in tiny concentric circles like a mini-whirlwind for about fifteen minutes, while he poured forth a continuous stream of prayer. The way he kept talking to the ceiling and mumbling my name made me think he was asking the Mayan gods directly for cleansing and healing. I was silent, focusing on the constriction in my head, wishing and hoping there was some way out this blackness. Periodically, I stared into the glasses of water. Sometimes I saw images pass through, animal creatures like I'd seen in my dream after the surfing accident, but mostly I saw a distorted reflection of myself.

After some time, Joselo gently placed the egg on the table

beside the first glass of water and picked up a second egg. He repeated the entire process, remaining focused in prayer, and placed the second egg next to its corresponding glass of water. I felt calm, my nervous system was quiet. He completed the ceremony by applying another dose of agua florída, this time a more liberal amount, and I felt the cool fragrant liquid drip down my neck and chest. I watched him reach for the white candles, to clean off my electromagnetic field, but now I was losing hope because my head was still pounding, my brain still faltering. The ceremony had lasted about forty minutes.

Joselo knelt down to crack open the eggs, carefully depositing them into their respective glasses of water. He explained that not only did he use the eggs for healing, he also used them to do a special reading. He cracked open the first. I watched it settle to the bottom of the glass, leaving a few bubbles and opaque streaks in its wake. As he cracked open the second, I felt a slight release in my head, as if I had been "uncorked." What looked like a giant spit wad rose to the surface, leaving a cloudy haze in the water. Joselo gasped. "Someone has throw you bad medicine," he said, pointing into the glass. "You see, it looks like someone spit on you!"

He told me that bubbles indicated guardian angels and the spit wad was blocking my connection with Spirit. I wondered when I might have been besieged by bad medicine, but my mind was spinning and I couldn't think. The pressure in my head, however, had diminished, so while my mind doubted the encounter, my body experienced some very real effects. Within ten minutes my head was completely clear and free of pain. As I walked out his front door I heard myself ask, "Will you teach me?"

Joselo explained that my body would be releasing toxins, or poisons, and that I might not feel well for a few days.

I was not prepared for how severe it got. Back in Antigua,

barely able to make it up the stairs to my motel room and into the bathroom, I spent the night on the bathroom floor, alternating between vomiting and diarrhea. My body was confused, one moment shivering and chilled to the bone, the next feverish and sweating. I rode the pain, taking breaks when my body allowed, preparing for the next round, amazed at how my body was automatically doing its own work of releasing toxins.

At dawn, the violence subsided. Grateful for a reprieve, I crawled into bed fully clothed, teeth chattering, head pounding, and curled into a fetal position, hoping I could sleep. But the pain in my lower back and stomach was unbearable; I remained mostly awake but unable to move for almost twenty-four hours. There I lay, empty and alone, wishing for the comfort of a familiar face, a gentle touch, a warm kiss. But there was only me.

Chapter 8

CLEANING HOUSE

Once I recovered from the purging, I remembered my promise and prepared to head back up to the lake to begin my training, to study the Mayan way. I was fascinated by the egg ceremony and wanted to learn more. Was it possible that Joselo had unleashed an energy that had been stored in my body? If so, how did it get there? I recalled how disoriented I'd felt that morning ten years ago, when the headaches first started, as if I'd awoken in someone else's body. What did it mean to be thrown bad medicine? Did it involve spells or witchcraft or some form of black magic? Maybe this was why I'd been led to Joselo. I retained a degree of skepticism, though, uncertain whether I really believed this story, or was merely clinging to the belief that I should.

Joselo had no phone, so I hopped on a bus and began the three-hour ride back up to Atitlán. It was just after dawn and the air was crisp and cold, my breath depositing tiny clouds of steam on the icy windows. I cupped my hands around a cup of hot coffee and watched the early-morning sun pop its head over the mountains, gently gracing the land with its presence. Groves of trees flicked by as the bus roared through the mountains. Occasionally, I'd see a man walking on the side of the road, hauling a heavy load of firewood on his back.

Arriving in Santiago, I walked along the same path I'd traversed several days before, smelling the same peppery herbs, until I reached Joselo's house. I called to him from the front door, and soon he was there on the step, greeting me with a warm smile, easing my anxiety. I told him that I had been in bed for several days, recuperating, but was now ready to learn whatever he would teach me.

"Yes, much to learn, but we have no hurry," he said, flashing an almost childlike smile. "I teach you, but first you must have cleansing with herbs. You must purify. This necessary you to make stronger your intuition."

I considered his words. "I take care of my body, I keep it as healthy as possible, but how is cleansing the body related to developing intuition?"

Joselo laughed. "Because it through body that we connect with Great Spirit, House of the World. You see, each person is tiny piece of World House," he said. "When we take sick, something in World House-Earth Body not working so good. The way to make better the body is to remember the whole house. You must make stronger your intuition, open to subtler realms."

"Subtler realms?" I asked. Through my study of yoga and Eastern philosophy, I understood much about cleansing, purifying, and the subtler realms, but wasn't yet clear whether the Mayans assigned similar meaning or held a different perspective.

Joselo continued, "There many realms, many layers. We live now in fifth layer. But we must wake up to others realms, to four layers before this one. You see, this how we enter the World House. So we must cleanse and purify: mind, body, soul. For you, we start with the herbs—like baptism, to begin peel the layers."

"But how do you know where to start?" I asked.

"I start where intuition tells me start. No more questions," he said gently. "Now, you have clothes, toothbrush?"

"I brought enough to last a few days," I said. "The rest is in Antigua."

"Good. You stay with us while you begin herbs," he said. "In case you get stuck, we bring you back home."

"Stuck?" I asked, forgetting I wasn't supposed to be asking questions. "Where would I get stuck?"

"Anywhere," he said with a smile. "Anywhere at all."

The next day Joselo and I headed to the marketplace to collect the ingredients for my cleansing: a bundle of roses, incense, tobacco, alcohol, and a variety of local herbs. He clearly was revered in the community. Several people gathered as we passed, and no one let us pay for anything, but I still didn't understand his role as the community doctor.

"I am spirit doctor," he said, amused by his own words. "I work on layer between human world and spirit world. Problems and sickness come as payment in spirit world, not human world."

"Payment?" I asked.

"Payment very important," he continued, "but not normal payment. Ritual is payment, way to remember and talk to the gods. You see, the gods need be fed. Then we can ask for healing."

"Do you think my health problems are related to spiritual payment?"

"Sí," he said. "Your horoscope tells of health problems. Illness is reminder you to dedicate to spiritual way, to Great Spirit. You have sensitive system, you are very lucky. This keep you honest, make easier your work."

That night, after cooking up an interesting concoction of flowers, herbs, and tobacco, I began my water cleansing, or the Pocomam way. Of course I didn't drink the tobacco that was included in the batch for my baths, but I drank a mixture of roses, herbs, and something I'm pretty sure was a sister to Ayahuasca, an intense hallucinogen. Joselo explained the regime I would follow for the next three weeks: "Each morning, you drink tea. Each night, you bathe in herbal water. During sleep, you leave body and soar through Universe."

I did as I was told, unsure whether to take him literally. After the first night, I had my answer. It felt as if in the nights I was downloading information onto my internal software, but I was able to retain only a small fraction of it. I knew that something was definitely happening, but for the life of me I couldn't remember any of these experiences—except one:

I have been transported across the country, to Tikal, somewhere deep in the Guatemalan jungle. I've never been here before, but somehow I'm familiar with the area. In my head I have a mental picture of the entire city, including all the buildings and structures. I still have my body, but I also have wings that allow me to fly. I hover above the city, using my inner radar to explore the ancient temples and pyramids, until I land at the top of temple IV. Here I sit, above the tallest trees of the jungle.

I become aware of the sound of heavy breathing, as if a thousand people are panting into a megaphone next to my ear. At first I'm bewildered. Where is this noise coming from? But then I know. It is coming from the ancient Mayans, the souls who had built these structures thousands of years ago. Now, the breathing is arising from within me, or perhaps I am flowing out of it, it seems to be one and the same. There is no separation between past and present, me and them—it's just happening.

I sit in the experience of breathing, somewhere out of time, witnessing the groundlessness of being.

The next day, I relayed my experience to Joselo.

"See!" he responded dramatically, "the spirits call you. You must keep open your ears, wait for message."

"I did—I will. But what does this mean?" I asked, feeling unnerved. Like the flying saucer incident at Hacienda Del Sol, I wanted to understand what all of this meant, what I was suppose to do with the information, how to apply it to my life. I was still waiting for all the pieces of the puzzle to fit neatly into place so I could rest. But why did I have a nagging suspicion that this might not happen?

"We must wait and see," Joselo whispered. "Only the spirits know answers to your question." Then he went back to his canvas; he was touching up the black hair of the woman he was painting, as though he hadn't been interrupted at all.

While evenings were reserved for astral travel or visiting the subtler realms—which was somewhat like intense, lucid dreaming, except there was a distinct unearthly quality to these experiences, as if other dimensions were coming up to meet me, ushering me through spiraling tunnels and wide open spaces and places that I had no reference for—I spent the following days studying the Mayan Science. Joselo thought it would be helpful to learn some of the technical points, so I could keep my mind occupied while my body went through its cleansing. This was a strategic move because while my mind was engaged in the minutiae of facts and figures, theoretically my body would be more receptive to the cleansing.

Joselo announced that I would begin by studying the Mayan calendar. "Mayan calendar is foundation for everything in Mayan world," he explained, "but it is only tiny drop in big sea of information. We start with the naguals."

"What are the naguals?" I asked.

"The Mayan calendar has twenty days, energies, called naguals." He spoke slowly so I could understand. He explained that each day also had a corresponding number, from one to thirteen, and that these twenty days and thirteen numbers continuously changed and overlapped but did not repeat until two hundred and sixty was reached. "You see?" he asked. "Thirteen times twenty? Two hundred and sixty days is how long our year."

"What is the significance of the numbers?" I asked.

"Numbers very important," he said. "Represent many things. You learn as we go."

Joselo explained that the human body has thirteen principle energy centers, the seven chakras and six others, and twenty genetic forces or whirlwinds, used to cleanse, balance, and regulate the system. Together, he said, these forces create energetic unity and wholeness, like that of the universe. He maintained that the twenty genetic forces and thirteen energy centers totaled the number thirty-three, that there are thirty-three vertebrae in human spine, and that each vertebra talks with one organ, completing a physical, emotional, spiritual, and energetic sphere.

"You see, everything in Mayan world important to whole organism," he said.

I looked at him, overwhelmed.

"Listen with inner ear," Joselo implored, searching my eyes to see if I could still follow him.

He went on to say that the Mayans believe that there is one

universe with three parts, a triune: the underworld, which is the intuitive realm and relates to numbers one through four; the world, which is about communication on the physical plane and corresponds with numbers five through eight; and the supra world, where everything is invisible and subtle and coincides with numbers nine through twelve. The number thirteen is reserved for God, Jesus, or a direct disciple.

"How do these numbers and energies differ from person to person?" I asked, trying to remember which ones I had seen in my horoscope.

Joselo smiled, indicating that I was catching on. "Horoscope show special energies and sacred numbers, this good. But we must look also what is missing. For you, no number eleven. Eleven is divine receptivity, ability to touch invisible realms. This difficult task. Eleven brings imbalance. For you, this makes health problems when you turn sideways from your spiritual path."

It was a lot to take in, especially when Joselo told me that the ancient Mayans had determined, using the patterns of the moon and their unique calendar, that this cycle of creation was to end on December 23, 2012, and that after that day everything would be different. This fascinated me and made me want to plunge in and study the history in depth. But I was aware, based on the success of the egg ceremony, that I might be a little too eager to adopt this information and treat it as gospel. I had recently recognized a tendency in myself to be a true believer. My inclination to believe tied in with the fantasy that there might actually be one right answer, one right person, or one right teaching that would mark the end of my search.

∞

One rainy night toward the end of June, after completing the first month of study, I sat alone on the cold tile floor in Joselo's house, lighting one candle for each of my nearly thirty-two years, and reflecting on my life. I thought back to the vision I'd had in the Osa. I regretted how harshly I'd treated myself in the past, how nothing I'd accomplished, materially or spiritually, was ever enough. I was still restless, still seeking, rarely stopping to appreciate what was. I thought about the man with the red head covering telling me I had many gifts to cultivate. But I knew that to cultivate these gifts, whatever they were, I'd have to let go of my limited ideas of how I thought things should go. I now had the opportunity to do things differently, to surrender my agenda and my expectations, and to really step into this experience. I didn't just want to go through the motions of being here. What would be the point? I wanted to make a truer commitment, a commitment to stop trying to figure out the mystery and allow it to unfold. Only then might I begin to access the deeper layers, or as the Mayans say, "The House of the World."

Believe me, I was ready.

Chapter 9

SHADOW SELF

One morning I returned from fishing with Joselo's three sons, to help cook and clean the house. This was how I paid for the teachings. His wife was there too—a chain-smoking, drastically underweight woman with long, stringy hair, also an artist—but her presence was hazy. She was usually sequestered in some tiny corner of the house or occasionally the garden, but she kept to herself. The family kept quite separate in their activities, though they usually shared meals, which consisted primarily of Coke, cold cuts, Wonder Bread, and the Guatemalan equivalent of Ding Dongs. To me, their fast food mentality seemed like a contradiction, especially in light of my required cleansing. And there were other contradictions. For instance, after a day of ceremonies and doctoring, Joselo would head to his bedroom to watch television. This was my shaman, the person who traveled to the spirit world and negotiated with the gods. The discrepancies bothered me. I held to a puritan ideology that said that spiritual seekers, and gurus in particular, were supposed to behave in a certain way, a way that was somehow holier than drinking Coke, smoking cigarettes, and watching TV. But I also knew that my judgments and opinions were self-limiting, that they were based in fear. When I could get past them I saw that the contradictions didn't matter, in fact focusing on them only served to keep me at a distance, separate. What mattered was a person's heart, and his integrity, and Joselo had both.

That morning we dumped the fish in the sink and I tried to go about my chores. The pressure in my head raged, a dark shadow lurking, threatening to annihilate an otherwise beautiful day. I thought I would do almost anything to rid myself of the pain, and yet, after a decade of sharing residence with this other, I was almost resigned to let it reign. Almost.

Joselo was on his way out the door to perform a fire ceremony in the mountains with another priest, but when he saw the glazed look in my eyes, he offered to perform an egg ritual to help me with the pain. His friend could wait.

I knew the ritual would provide only a temporary fix. As with my chiropractic adjustments, the egg ceremonies helped clear my head, increase my energy, and temporarily allow me to resume a normal routine. Invariably, the pain would then return, leaving me frustrated and confused, no closer to finding a real cure. Over the years this cycle had become debilitating, and I still judged myself harshly for being unable to fix the problem. But on this day I had a new insight: I noticed that when I was able to experience emotional pain, observe and feel it without trying to change it, the emotions eventually dissipated or transformed into something else. So, though tolerating incapacitating physical pain was another matter altogether, maybe I needed to stop battling, stop seeking relief, and just experience the discomfort. It seemed like an impossible task.

I surrendered into the now familiar ritual, but this time, when Joselo bent down to crack open the eggs, half of one of the shells landed in the glass, along with the yolk and a little speck of blood.

"Look!" he exclaimed. "There is trapped energy, hiding. Now it no escape. We must perform fire ceremony, before it goes back to sleep."

"What?" I asked irritably, my head still aching. "I don't understand about this trapped energy. I thought the eggs were supposed to release the toxins, now you want to do a fire ceremony? What's that for?"

Joselo was quiet, seemingly lost in thought. "You ask many questions," he said finally. "You came to learn, yes?"

"Yes," I said, "but I need to understand what you are doing and why."

"No, you need understand less and experience more. Understanding will come later. I say only this: there is trapped energy in your body, but is your own energy, your shadow. The attack come from inside out. Jun Q'anil, you must learn to tame internal demons, only then you will be free."

This statement struck a chord. I knew that this journey was about taming my demons, but so far, I hadn't thought of my physical challenges as an internal attack, as if one part of me was waging battle against another. What if what Joselo said was true? Could this enslaved aspect of myself be causing an internal war, in some way contributing to my own demise?

I sighed. "When should we perform this ceremony?"

"Now," he said. "Come. Ramon waits for us in Pana, we go to the mountains."

Who in the world was Ramon? I thought, as I hurried to follow Joselo out the door.

∞

After purchasing a liter of water and some fruit, we boarded a boat to Pana, where we got into an old VW van with Ramon and his wife, Yolanda. Joselo sat in front with Ramon's daughter on his lap, while I hopped in back beside Yolanda and the eight-month-old baby slung across her midsection. Yolanda had recovered from a car wreck in which she "broke her head" and survived seven days in a coma. The accident had happened one year before. I couldn't help but wonder if something had been forever lost. Her voice was barely audible and she looked only half-alive as she nervously nibbled a few strawberries, the child suckling at her bare breast. It was a huge effort for her to speak, and I watched as she periodically stared off into space, a look of great distress in her eyes. Like so many times throughout this journey, I was struck by the fragility of life.

After riding for an hour or so, we arrived in Chichicastenango, the town in which we would purchase the materials for our ceremony, including tobacco, alcohol, chocolate, incense, sugar, and a variety of herbs and candles, all to be used as offerings, or payment for the gods. I learned that this particular day was called oxlajuj toj, the day of payment.

"What does that mean?" I asked Joselo.

"Oxlajuj [thirteen] is transformational number, the messenger," he explained, "and toj is day of payment. You are lucky, this is strongest day for payment."

On this day, thirteen toj, or day of atonement, the Mayans believe that people must pay for their existence. Lucky or not, I was nervous when I watched Joselo and Ramon purchase two huge bags full of materials in preparation for our ceremony. I gathered there was a lot of payment to be made.

∞

There are hundreds of places around Guatemala and in the rest of the Mayan world that are considered especially sacred, places where the people go to perform their rituals and ceremonies. Some of these sites are designated as national parks or reserves, as in the case of Calakmul, Tikal, Copán, Palenque, Cobá, and several other ancient Mayan cities. Other cherished spots are hidden high in the mountains, often in caves or natural limestone cavern pools, but never in plain view.

We entered just past the ruins of K'umarcaaj. Ramon pulled over to the side of the road and the six of us collected our supplies and piled out of the van. The area was cool and heavily wooded and I wondered if the sweater I'd brought would keep me warm enough. Joselo wandered into the thicket and stopped in front of a small pile of smoldering ashes and a few unusual rocks. It was here that we must ask for permission to enter the area and perform our ceremony. If I hadn't been looking, I would have missed it entirely. I watched as Joselo knelt onto the earth and gently placed his lips upon the moist soil, showing his reverence for Mother Earth. He lit several candles and prayed, asking for permission to enter the sacred land. Ramon and Yolanda did the same. I too knelt down and lit a few candles, and asked for both permission and protection.

It was partly sunny as we began our trek up the mountain, but the rain wasn't far off. I watched in astonishment as Yolanda steadily made her way up the incline, baby and all. Ramon followed directly behind her, the other child sitting on his shoulders, several large packs on his back, and a gallon of water tucked under his arm. I noticed that Joselo had a slight limp; he'd injured his leg many years earlier, and before long was winded, stopping periodically to catch his breath. I appreciated his humanness in that moment, his vulnerability, the fact that he too had weaknesses. I offered to carry his load, in addition to mine, and he gratefully accepted.

An hour later we were halfway up. Gray clouds sealed the sky. I stopped to drink some water and take in the view, but mostly I absorbed the strangeness of it all, the fact that I was about to participate in a ceremony designed to expel unwanted energies, an exorcism. I looked at Ramon and Yolanda; like Joselo they seemed to be in their element, hiking up a mountain to partake in the ritual. I wanted to be in my element, to feel that this was my natural place, but I wasn't sure. Actually, I was annoyed that it was taking so long, I didn't know it would be a whole-day affair, and I was frustrated with myself for feeling mildly bored and impatient. Instead of judging, though, I tried to experience my resistance and continue walking.

Once at the top, I saw several small caves and scattered groups of people, each group gathered around their small fire. The men and women wore brightly colored clothing, and each seemed intently focused on a particular task: setting up materials, tending the fire, praying, washing, lighting candles. Joselo explained that throughout the country, in the hundreds of small villages, the weave of the cloth, the color of the clothing, and the way it was worn was a visual signifier of regions, dialects, marital status, spiritual position, and various other bits of information. Here on top of the mountain was no different.

We found a place under the overhang of a small cave, sheltered from the coming rain. Joselo cleaned the area, sweeping away branches and debris, and lit candles toward the rear of the cave, again asking the spirits for permission to occupy their space. He instructed me to light one candle in each of the four directions and clarify my intention for the ceremony. The only reason I was there was because half an eggshell had fallen into the glass—an odd reason to be on the top of a mountain, moments away from entering a Mayan sacrament. But I remembered Joselo's words: "Attack come from inside out." I dedicated the ceremony to my complete physical, emotional, and spiritual healing, though without too many expectations. I asked for clarity on my path, set my intention, lit the candles, and gave thanks. When it started to rain, lightly at first and then more heavily, I was grateful for our little cave.

When Joselo saw me watching a group of people to my right, sacrificing a chicken, he instructed me not to look. Even though the Spaniards had banned ritual human sacrifice in the sixteenth century, many Mayans still practiced animal blood sacrifice to achieve the same end—another form of payment.

"Why shouldn't I look?" I asked.

Joselo explained that it wasn't the looking itself that could get me into trouble; rather, the looking could generate fear, and fear could create an opening in my aura through which negative energy could enter. To guard against that possibility, everyone donned red head coverings to protect the crown chakra and placed a red cloth around the belly to insulate the second chakra.

We began to arrange our materials into a designated circle that Joselo had carefully prepared. First the sugar was used to outline the border, next we laid down the incense, herbs, and tobacco, each a form of payment toward our good fortune. Joselo instructed us to position our candles, each of the four colors corresponding with one of the four directions, one of the four elements, and one of the four balams, or sacred gods.

He spoke: "The white candles go to north, god of air. The yellow candles go to south, god of water. The red candles go to east, god of fire. The black candles go to west, god of earth."

Despite my presumptions about rituals, that they were basically a lot of form over substance, I was moved by Joselo's devotion, the way he gently placed each candle, how he lovingly conversed with the gods, how through single-minded attention he was able to transform ordinary tasks into sacred events, like a Zen master taking a walk in the woods. The emphasis was on being present instead of achieving results, which, while contrary to my habitual way of operating, was exactly what I needed in order to suspend judgment and begin to embrace what was happening.

Once the candles were in place and everyone was ready, Joselo initiated another round of prayer and lit the fire. He spoke mostly in his native Quiché. I couldn't understand what he said, but was able to absorb the tone. It seemed that this circle, approximately three feet in diameter, held the space for some very intense energy. Joselo called upon the four directions, the four elements, and the four sacred gods, as well as the past, the present, and the future, initiating a trip into time and space whereby anything was possible.

He called upon the twenty sacred energies, or naguals, and the thirteen numbers, paying special attention to the energy of the day, oxlajuj toj, the day of payment. He asked to make the darkness light, to elevate our consciousness, and for each of us to be in harmony with God. Through our offerings we paid for our family, our community, and our existence, and in return asked for clarity, a deeper connection with the Divine. This day marked a new beginning.

Joselo motioned for me to approach the fire and assume a wide-legged stance. I felt the familiar agua florída trickle down my spine as I watched him use his pixom' kakol, or sacred bundle, to cleanse my body. "Concentrate," he whispered. "Make attention like laser. You must die to fire and receive your healing."

I knew it was time to let go of the fears that were no longer serving me: my controlling nature, my obsessive worrying, my compulsive need to know, but I wasn't sure how. I wanted to trust this process, to embrace the opportunities that were presenting themselves, but it was hard to let go of my deeply ingrained patterns. Sanda had said that the only way to change a self-defeating behavior was to take a different action, to stand up to our fears. Right now, I knew that standing up to my fear meant surrendering even further, to admit that I didn't know. I didn't know how to heal my body, quiet my mind, or satisfy my insatiable desire to know. I certainly hadn't a clue what I was doing in the mountains of Guatemala, standing over a fire, a Mayan shaman sprinkling strange liquids down my back, rubbing eggs on my body, and telling me to ask the gods for help. But, undeniably, I was here. Somehow I'd been led to the unusual man, and I wanted to make the most of it. I remained focused on the fire and entered a light trance.

I am motionless, rooted, as part of me drifts away from the world of form and into the fire. I am being suctioned through a long light-filled tunnel, weightlessly tumbling about, until there is nothing but wide-open space. I feel like an astronaut looking down from a spaceship, where I have an unobstructed view of planet Earth rotating on its axis. Suddenly, I begin to laugh uncontrollably, cackling like a hyena, but I don't know what I am laughing at. Everything is just absurdly funny. The laughter feels like sweet medicine, and I become instantly peaceful.

A clap of thunder broke the spell, returning me to my body. Disoriented, I looked around to find Joselo and the others talking quietly, a light smoke replacing what had once been our fire. How long had I been gone? I felt a little awkward, since I didn't know these people and I'd just been laughing my head off for no reason in particular. But I figured they understood. I had become more comfortable exploring the unknown realms and even found a sense of peace there. But it wasn't enough. The next step was to integrate this kind of peace in my everyday life, regardless of where I was or what fears arose. And I hoped to become more intimate with the source behind it.

∞

Iawoke the next morning with a desire to sit and do nothing.
The ceremony had zapped every last bit of energy I possessed.
Thoughts passed through my mind like the early morning fog
that crept along the lake's surface.

Joselo found me sitting outside. "How was ceremony?" he
asked.

"Intense," I said. "Even the muscles in my face are tired."

He grinned. "Yes, but you have new awareness, no?"

He was right. I had seen and felt that many other dimensions
existed simultaneously, and that reality as I knew it wasn't the
main attraction. But would this awareness help to transform my
life? I wondered if my life even needed to be transformed.

He smiled. "You have questions?"

I always had questions. "What did you mean when you said
the attack has come from the inside out?"

"You no in harmony with your essence for many years,
yes?"

I nodded.

"You are breaking free from yourself. This very powerful.
Attack has come at your essence, force you to transform, or
die. So far you survived, but with much difficulty. This reason
for your head pains."

"But why?" I asked.

"There no other way, it was written in planets. Attack will
make you woman you must become, and teacher for others. Not
easy. The universe had to make sure you ready."

"Great," I said. "Did I pass?"

"You almost finished. I think maybe few more years."

"What? I can't possibly withstand a few more years."

"Yes, you will do it. No choice." Joselo said.

I was so tired, suddenly feeling the weight of the past several years—the headaches, the searching, the energy it took to hold things together when really I wanted to fall apart. A part of me wanted to give up and go home. I recalled a recent dream in which my entire body was cut up and bleeding as I ran naked from my mother's house. I told Joselo.

"Part of you dying, coming apart," he said. "You run from the old life, the mother's house. But you must take care. It is not good you go back to old life. It is time you go somewhere new, maybe here, no?"

"I want to go back," I said, "but I know it's not time yet."

"You are right, it is not time. First you must walk the Camino."

I looked to Joselo.

He explained that the Camino, or the Fire way, is the path of enlightenment for a Mayan priest. This sacrifice, walking to sacred sites and performing sacred ceremonies for the benefit of all beings, is how the Mayans honor and communicate with the gods.

"The Camino no easy," he said. "Many years of training. But it will make strong your core. If you develop ability, you will become Quiché Mayan priest, very honorable, and you will serve others."

I was intrigued, yet something told me to proceed with caution.

"Once initiated as priest," Joselo continued, "you may stay here or return to your country, but you may not give up responsibility. The spirits will not allow."

"I need to think about this," I said.

"Yes, you think." Joselo smiled. "There is no hurry."

Chapter 10

SYNCHRONICITY

To gain some perspective, I decided to head back to Antigua. I rented a loft that faced a small inner courtyard, home to one of the loveliest gardens I had ever seen. With many of the properties in Antigua—which for security reasons are more like sealed compounds, with twenty-to-thirty-foot walls circling their perimeters—the garden is vital, usually located smack in the center. This garden was impeccably manicured, with climbing plants, ferns, bromeliads, and several kinds of orchids, including the rare monja blanca (white nun orchid). There were also small avocado and lemon trees toward the rear. Orange bougainvillea, a color I'd seldom seen, inched its way up the surrounding stucco walls.

From the loft I had a perfect view of Fuego, an active volcano, and of an archway in the neighboring ruins—a picture inside a picture. Each morning I watched the birds glide through the arch against the backdrop of powder-blue sky. I unpacked the suitcases I had been lugging around for months and headed to the market for fruits and vegetables: apples, bananas, papayas, tomatoes, avocados, cucumbers, beans, corn, and rice, most of which had to be soaked in a tub of water with a teaspoon of Clorox bleach to kill the parasites. I also bought four dozen roses, a dollar a dozen, to help make the place feel like home. And since I'd been taking cold baths for several months, I immediately took a hot shower. I cut my hair, scrubbed my body, and cooked up a big pot of vegetable soup. I gave away many of my clothes, sent the rest out for laundering, and bought myself a wool quechquemitl, a traditional Guatemalan shoulder cape, to keep warm at night. I tried to construct the semblance of a normal life, though there was nothing normal about it.

Maybe it was the fact that despite my attempt to create a comfortable, homey atmosphere and ward off my encroaching doubts—doubts that perhaps I was fooling myself, that I was trying to create something out of nothing—I felt ungrounded and confused. Not that this process should feel good; I knew this experience might be uncomfortable and disorienting, but I kept wishing it wasn't. I still wanted things to be other than they were, I wanted comfort, confirmation, instant enlightenment. Somehow these ideal states seemed more acceptable than my messy confusion. But now, I'd found the shaman and the fire, a promise of clear direction finally in plain view.

And yet, something was amiss.

Was I prepared to take this escapade to the next level and become a Mayan priest? Did it really suit me? If not, should I go home? I knew I hadn't uncovered the mystery—sure, I'd had lots of insights and interesting experiences, but I hadn't found the peace I was looking for. I did notice, however, that I had put aside my trusty anchors, yoga and meditation, attempting to replace them with the Mayan way. I found myself looking to Joselo for the answers, elevating him to a godly level, placing all my faith into him and his teachings to the exclusion of my own ideas. These must be the teachings that would bring forth a transformation, I thought, or why would I have been guided here?

I had once read that a student of consciousness should choose one discipline to study in depth. If she does not, she remains like an animal in search of water, tasting from many shallow puddles, but never able to drink from her source. Maybe it didn't matter which discipline I studied, as long as I chose one. I remembered a quote from a Zen master: "You must burn all your bridges so you can never go back."

Even though the Mayan way didn't completely resonate, if it was time to burn my bridges, this was as good a place as any. Besides, the opportunity was right in front of me. I considered the fact that the Mayan way provided a means to attain enlightenment, a clear and specific path. The teachings and rituals were fascinating, often rendering stupendous results, and yet the way in which they were practiced felt to me almost formulaic, rote. Maybe I just needed to give it some time.

For days I sat in the town's center square, absorbing the sunshine and the local scene, staring at the Catedral de Santiago, an ornate sixteenth-century church that had only been partially rebuilt after the 1773 earthquake. I watched the Mayan women carting their colorful handmade crafts upon their heads—purses, headbands, blankets—and flashing their silver-toothed smiles. I sat amidst the comings and goings, hoping to glean some insight into my own life. I spent the nights in tiny cafes, drinking tea and listening to Latin music, while the rain turned the bricks a rusty red. Occasionally, I'd share a meal with another traveler, but mostly I ate alone, a spectator suspended between two worlds. I was getting ready to make the ultimate decision, whether or not to become a Quiché Mayan priest.

I awoke one morning, tired and nauseated, my stomach moving and gurgling, distended to twice its normal size, feeling like it was full of shaving cream; it seemed whatever was in my belly had siphoned all my reserves. I was bedridden for a week. Throughout, Doña Della, the woman who owned the loft, took my temperature and offered me warm drinks. Her best guess was that I had ingested a parasite or some amoebas, but it could also be hepatitis B. Either way, I needed to see a doctor, but finding a suitable one in Guatemala isn't easy under the best circumstances, let alone when one is barely able to move. I waited, sleeping often, taking short breaks to read or write, hoping that whatever had taken up residence in my stomach would either die or pass through my intestines.

I thought about Joselo, his commitment to work and family, his dedication to the Mayan way. He seemed to have the ability to flow through life as if nothing could disturb his inner peace. This was the quality I most admired.

At the end of the week, I heard a knock at the door. Joselo stood there, grinning, dressed in plain clothes. I welcomed him into my home.

"You look not so good," he said.

"So I've heard."

Joselo smiled. "I know doctor in the city, maybe we go visit."

"But how did you know where to find me?" I asked.

"You no understand the power of mind? You called me here, same how I called you to Guatemala."

"You mean that by thinking about you, I was sending you my address?"

"Sí," he said. "People think it only coincidence, but this happens all the time. You see, thoughts are energy and energy can go anywhere in universe." He lifted his hand to the sky and twirled it around. "When we make intuition strong and learn how to use, we pick up more subtle energy."

"So you know I'm sick?" I asked.

"Yes. We will visit my wife's grandmother, Ursula. She is good doctor. Ursula is old and very stubborn, she no agree with nobody, but she has knowledge of many things. Go now, collect your things, and bring photo of you. She will need photo to do diagnosis."

"A photograph?" I asked "For a diagnosis?"

"This no time to start with your questions. Now go!"

Ursula worked out of her home, a small apartment on Avenida Reforma, Zona 9, in the heart of Guatemala City. I wondered how she could tolerate the noise and pollution. Then I remembered I had spent the majority of my life walking through the smog-filled streets of Los Angeles. I guess it's all a matter of what we're used to. Her place was simple, decorated with mismatched furniture from the 1970s: a red vinyl couch; two high-back upholstered chairs, one orange and the other green; a shabby rug; and Formica-topped tables. No less than ten academic and honorary degrees hung on her living room walls. At eighty, Ursula had an imposing presence, one that demanded immediate respect—Joselo was right—but she greeted me with a sort of vacant smile; she seemed to look through me rather than at me. It was as if some crucial part of her were missing, or lost. Her eyes spoke of a deep sadness, I thought then, but later learned that Ursula had cataracts and could barely see. "What can I do for you?" she asked, all business.

I had no idea how to answer her question, maybe because I felt sick and utterly forlorn. Nonetheless, for some reason I felt inclined to unload my entire life story, right there on her red vinyl couch, as if the telling would provide a healing in itself. Not that I hadn't told my story enough times, but somehow I sensed that Ursula could help, that she might provide another piece of the puzzle.

"Joselo tells me you're not feeling well," she continued before I had time to answer her initial question.

"Yes," I said, relieved that she spoke decent English. "My stomach's been hurting for a week and I have no appetite."

Ursula nodded and went to fetch something from the other room. I watched her walk down the hall in her kelly-green Ditto jeans and black ballet slippers. Her spine tilted slightly forward, and her long arms, almost too long for her body, hung like fishing lures by her side. She moved with a kind of purposeful concentration, as if while in transit she was working out something in her mind.

Ursula returned holding a piece of paper that had the numbers one to one hundred fifty written in long columns across the page. Taking my hand, she took out a pendulum, a copper arrow dangling from a chain, and used it to scan the page, stopping at each number. Sometimes the pendulum would circle to the right, sometimes to the left, and sometimes it would do nothing. After scribbling a few notes, she announced that I had contracted amoebas. "Guardia," she said evenly. "They're ugly creatures. Under a microscope they look like little screaming ghosts."

"But how do you know I have amoebas?" I asked.

"The way I sense disorder in the body is by tuning into vibration," Ursula explained. "The pendulum helps me to measure minute vibrational interactions within a person that may be causing problems. And if I don't have the patient in front of me, I'll use a photograph to establish resonance with that person's energy field. This is how I diagnose and treat people. Usually, I catch whatever is present at the time of examination, but occasionally I'll identify problems that haven't manifested, but may develop in the future, like early detection of cancer or HIV."

"I see. And how would you recommend I get rid of the amoebas?"

"You can take a strong antibiotic that will kill all the healthy microorganisms in your body, but may not touch the guardia. Or you can spend ten minutes on the machine."

"What machine?" I asked.

"I have a machine that will kill the amoebas but not the rest of you," she said.

I looked to Joselo for confirmation.

"If you remember back to your basic science class," Ursula continued, "you remember that two negatives create a positive. By using a low level of electricity, the machine enables me to match the rate of vibration of diseased or foreign microorganisms, causing them to explode and die, while the healthy microorganisms are preserved."

"So the machine can kill the amoebas?" I asked.

"Yes. But I think we should do a full diagnosis. I sense your system is severely compromised."

I wasn't sure I wanted to know about any potential problems. I already had more than I could handle. "Let's just eliminate the amoebas," I said.

"As you wish."

Ursula ushered me into another room where I met her assistant, Mercedes, who sat me down next to a small apparatus that looked like an old radio from the 1950s. Into my hands, Mercedes carefully tucked two metal receptors that projected from the machine, and she placed my feet on a small sheet of aluminum. Even before she turned on the power, I could feel a slight vibration. When she switched the dial to on, my body jolted as a strong wave of electricity coursed through my veins. She adjusted the "volume" until I was able to sit still and feel the current. It was not pleasant, but it wasn't exactly unpleasant either.

Three days and one more treatment later, all my symptoms had disappeared. I took the bus back to Ursula's house, this time without Joselo, to confirm that there was nothing lingering. With her finger on my photograph, Ursula used her pendulum to scan the "Amoeba and Parasite" section on her paper. This time the instrument was still; there was no longer activity there.

"Amazing," I said. "Do people in the States know about this?"

"Not many," she said. "The machine was built in the United States, but its use has been prohibited. Perhaps it poses too great a threat to the healthcare industry. The machine is simple. We program the frequency, establish the length of time needed, and turn it on. The challenge is to properly diagnose and determine the appropriate frequency, otherwise the treatment is useless."

"Can anyone learn how to do this?" I asked.

She glanced wistfully at a large photograph of an elderly man opposite her desk. She suddenly had that absent stare, as if engaged in a daydream that was more real to her than anything here.

"Is that your husband?" I asked.

"Yes, that was Henry," she said. It was clear she didn't want to talk about her personal life. "Tell me how you found Joselo," she asked.

I told her everything about our meeting, from beginning to end, and that I was now in the process of making a big decision.

"Has your time together been beneficial?" she asked.

"Yes, very," I said. "And yet I have reservations about making the next level of commitment to become a Mayan priest."

Ursula fell silent, scanning me, as if trying to assess whether she should state her opinion or leave me to figure things out on my own. When she spoke again her voice was clear and still. "Think about this decision very carefully. Pay attention to your doubts."

I thought back to the ceremony in which I asked for my complete physical, emotional and spiritual healing. Well, here I was, sitting with what appeared to be an extraordinary healer. In spite of my fear that she might detect some rare terminal illness, or even worse, that I was destined to live with mysterious head pains the rest of my life, I decided to have Ursula do her full diagnosis. It seemed unlikely that she would discover anything new, yet I had been delivered to her doorstep. Perhaps, as Joselo had suggested, our life encounters were not coincidental. It seemed that when I surrendered my agenda, the universe was still there to support me. Just perhaps, everything *was* going according to plan.

Chapter 11

MAXIMÓN

I made it back to Antigua by dusk. I took a steaming mug of tea and climbed up to the roof of my loft. A shadow had fallen across the purple mountains, behind them the setting summer sun. Intermittent puffs of smoke emerged from the neighboring volcano, making the clouds appear as streaks of silver strewn across the lavender sky. I inhaled and felt a sense of calm. Twilight was a special time in Antigua.

I remained there as twilight blended into night. I tried to imagine my life in Guatemala, learning the language, studying the culture, performing the Mayan ceremonies. I was fascinated by all of it, but wasn't sure I could make it my own. The ceremonies were difficult, they required a disciplined mind; the whole endeavor felt like a lot of effort, but Joselo had said that hard work was the very thing I needed to right my imbalance. Not psychological work so much, though that was part of it. Rather, I needed to dedicate myself to truly sacrificial work—not because I enjoyed it, but because it would benefit others. It was a larger call, as he put it, and I think that was partly true: authentic transformation was not about what I wanted, but more the death of the wanter.

I thought about Ursula, too, who in her uniquely abrupt way might also be a crucial teacher. I sensed that beneath her cool exterior was a woman who possessed a lot of wisdom. In addition to whatever might be discovered through her treatments, I wanted to pick her brain, to learn how she came upon her methods, discover the root of what inspired her. And perhaps there would be other surprises in Guatemala, other resources and experiences. Maybe I would even grow to appreciate my training, finally surrendering the stubborn ego and serving others, no longer from the perspective of my little self, but by tapping into Great Spirit. Maybe it was time for me to stop questioning and trust that I was where I needed to be, doing what I needed to do. And so, as the sun rose the next morning, I made my decision. I would walk the Camino and become a Quiché Mayan priest.

When Joselo heard about my decision, he made plans for us to visit the house of Maximón to perform a ceremony and ask for a blessing. There is a long complicated history behind Maximón (pronounced MAH-shee-MOHN), a local deity who is probably a blend of ancient Maya gods, Pedro de Alvarado, the fierce conquistador of Guatemala, and the biblical Judas. As a result, all the different statues of Maximón erected throughout the country have slightly different faces.

Joselo and I took the bus from Antigua to the neighboring village of Iztapa, where we purchased our materials for the ceremony—flowers, candles, incense, tobacco, the usual stuff. The day was a scorcher. We slowly wound our way up the cobblestone streets toward the highest peak in the city. I was grateful for the long white cirrus clouds that fanned across the indigo sky; the direct sun would have been unbearable in our heavy clothes and head coverings. From a distance, the house of Maximón looked like a small country church, with stark white walls and several long steps leading up to the main entrance.

As we approached the property, I noticed a few Mayan priests standing out front, each tending a separate fire. I learned that fire ceremonies were performed every day throughout the Mayan world, when priests and shamans traveled to the mountains, often on behalf of someone in their community, to perform the sacred rituals and ask the gods for healing. Joselo explained that it was the priest's job to determine which day had the appropriate energetic components for a particular ceremony.

"How does that work?" I asked.

"Today is oxlajuj q'anil," Joselo began, "powerful day. Q'anil is day you were born, it is seed of new life, new beginnings. It is good day to begin project, take trip, get pregnant. Oxlajuj is transformational number, the messenger. Today anything is possible. Over time you make intuition about the energies. I think you will be good priest."

"But will anyone take me seriously?" I asked, wondering if I could take myself seriously in this role. I doubted the Indians would accept a white woman into their community, and I wondered how this teaching might translate in the States, how it would work to perform fire ceremonies in the Santa Monica Mountains. It would be a fire hazard, if not illegal. I liked the idea, though; it held a kind of romance, a kind of mystery, but there again it was just my ego fantasizing.

"After some time," Joselo said, "when you learn Quiché dialect and others see you know the way, then you will gain respect. But you no worry about this now."

I glanced at my reflection in the window, a red cloth wrapped around my head and a matching red sash around my belly. I was still questioning it all.

"Today," Joselo continued, "I will introduce you to Maximón. You must ask for permission to walk the Camino and receive blessing."

"How will I know if I have been granted permission?"

"You will know," Joselo assured me. "There will be sign."

The interior of the house we entered was filled with dark smoky ash. Instead of church pews, long tables had been set up where visitors lit candles, burned incense, and smoked tobacco in an effort to pay homage to the holy man. Armed with roses and money, people stood in line waiting to kiss the feet of his life-sized statue, which sat stoically at the front of the room. Everyone was in a focused state of reverence, much like I had seen in churches, temples, and meditation halls throughout the world. The walls were adorned with gold plaques and inscribed with blessings, testimonials of Maximón's miraculous healings.

"Introduce yourself," Joselo urged. "Go light your candles and begin to pray."

I hesitated. How could I introduce myself to a statue of a man I didn't know or feel any connection with? I suppose I could pretend, but what would be the point? I might never truly integrate with the people or their avatar, much like I'd never felt connected to Christianity or Judaism or Islam. In principle I understood that a deified statue, whether Jesus, Buddha, or Maximón, was there to help us remember our Divine Nature, regardless of the name we chose to call it. But I'd always had trouble talking to inanimate objects. I needed to feel it within myself.

"Speak to him like you speak to your highest self," Joselo suggested. "Ask that he show you the way. Take the time you need, I wait outside."

I watched Joselo leave. Then I found a little niche where there weren't too many people and I lit a few candles. I began to concentrate on my deep yoga breathing, hoping this would calm the critical thoughts declaring this all a big charade. As I began to meditate, the surroundings slowly faded into the background. My body felt lighter and lighter, as if the months of journeying had sufficiently worn down my psyche so I could access these deeper states more easily. Suddenly, I was traveling through the familiar light-filled tunnel, but instead of being deposited into wide-open space like the time before, I found myself situated near a young child's birthday party.

I am in the backyard of a small house. There are about ten eight-year-olds running around with a ball, shrieking and yelling. Ten chairs are set out in a circle on the lawn, each with a brightly colored balloon attached to one of its legs. Inside there are a few women, cooking and laughing, preparing lunch for the children. I catch the eye of one woman, but she appears not to see, and I wonder if I'm invisible to all these people.

One of the children approaches me. He is the birthday boy, an angelic child with almond eyes and sandy curls. It seems he is the only one who can see me. In a short exchange, he says his name is David and that today he is eight years old. Remembering the journeying exercises with Sanda in which I learned inwardly to communicate with people and animals, I ask him, "Do you have something to show me?"

He nods yes.

"What is it?" I ask, aware how easily this moment could be lost or interrupted.

David peers at me. Without breaking eye contact, he slowly reaches out to take my hand. Inside his left palm is etched a six-pointed blue star, the Star

of David. I look back into his amber eyes.
  "Bye," he says, waving.
  "Bye," I say. And the scene dissolves.

When I came back to awareness, I didn't know how much time had passed or whether Joselo would still be waiting outside. It seemed weird that I'd have a vision of a Jewish star here under Maximón's reign, but then again, I wasn't necessarily looking for things to make sense. I recited a short prayer to the statue, lit a few candles, and headed for the door. When I stepped outside, the light hit me like a starburst. I grabbed onto the wall to steady myself, relieved to find Joselo right where he said he'd be, socializing with another priest. I told him about my vision.

"Let us see what this reveals," he said smiling mischievously. "Now, we must perform ceremony." He began to prepare the site.

Joselo led us through a fire ceremony similar to the one I had attended in the mountains. He explained that during the months ahead we would travel to many sacred places to perform these rituals, and eventually I would need to complete thirteen of them on my own. But on this day he asked only for the gods to light my way.

By the time we had finished, the late afternoon sun was so strong, tiny beads of sweat had gotten caught in the crevices of my charcoal-stained face. Joselo and I collected our belongings and walked into the little pueblo in search of a cold drink and a light meal. I felt unusually peaceful, and when the villagers looked up from their work to see us pass, I felt comfortable gazing directly into their eyes. It was well past midday but not yet suppertime, so Joselo ducked into a small storefront and asked the women if they would still serve us lunch. He motioned for me to follow him.

I stopped off in the kitchen to say hello to the women, practicing the little Quiché dialogue I was learning, feeling odd, as if I had been there before. Somehow the women looked familiar. I rejoined Joselo and followed him outside to a small patio. Soon we were standing in the middle of a young child's birthday party, complete with chairs and balloons and a smattering of kids running around the yard. I looked back to the storefront, which also doubled as a house, and watched the women cooking our lunch in their kitchen. That's when things started to move in slow motion, as if I was straddling two worlds, seeing into another layer.

Joselo, who'd heard my vision, looked surprised too. I lowered myself down in one of the chairs and tried to orient myself. I scanned the yard for the young boy, David. I was almost relieved that he wasn't there—until I spotted a child running from the outhouse, anxious to rejoin the party. It was he, sandy curls and all. I sat frozen.

Joselo ordered our lunch: chicken, beans, and rice with a side of handmade corn tortillas and two giant Cokes. I kept my eye on David, mesmerized by his every move. When the kids settled down in the yard, I watched him find his chair. Here was my chance. I walked steadily across the yard. David sensed me approach and he looked up, exposing those beautiful almond eyes. It seemed we had a moment of recognition. I sat down on the ground beside his small chair and began to speak with him in Spanish. He told me that his name was David. This was his eighth birthday party.

"Wonderful," I said. "Are you having fun?"

He nodded. He told me that this was the house of his cousin,

Pablo, and that he actually lived in a neighboring pueblo. I asked
if he had anything special to show me.

He smiled. Then he gently raised his left hand and opened his
palm. And there it was, the six-pointed Star of David. I inhaled
sharply as he laughed playfully.

"Wow," I said, trying to act nonchalant. "How long have you
had that star on your hand?"

"Forever," he said matter-of-factly.

"Yes, of course" I said. "Forever indeed."

W hen I returned to our table, Joselo said that he had seen
the star.

"What do you think it means?" I asked. Was my dead grandmother sending me a message? Was this a sign that I should go
home and study Jewish mysticism instead? The idea of jumping
on a plane and heading off to temple didn't feel right to me.

"The star, no sé, but you have your answer," Joselo said.

"My answer?"

"Yes, I told you once you made visit with Maximón and asked
for permission to walk the Camino you would receive sign. This
is it. The way is now open."

Joselo's certainty that I had been granted permission by the
"powers that be" seemed questionable—I didn't think a Jewish
star in a Catholic country held much significance. But I did agree
that the whole encounter was bizarre, and very moving.

I looked out to the yard and watched David playing with his
friends. He was just an eight-year-old boy enjoying his birthday party. He and I exchanged brief smiles. I drained the last
sip of Coke from the bottle, trying to figure out how all these
pieces might eventually come together.

Chapter 12

DIVINE INTERVENTION

During the next two months, I divided my time between studying with Joselo up at the lake and traveling into Guatemala City to undergo treatment with Ursula. Her full diagnosis had confirmed that my system was indeed compromised. Using her pendulum and her ability to tune into vibration, Ursula detected a blockage in my spinal cord that, when taxed, restricted the oxygen blood supply to my brain. This, she hypothesized, was the culprit behind my severe head pain and loss of energy. Also, she determined that my pituitary gland was inactive, as were my pineal and thyroid glands, all of which contributed to the absence of my menstrual periods. "I think this has less to do with an old eating disorder and more to do with taking the birth control pills for ten years," she said.

I stared at her in disbelief.

She went on. "The pill sends commands to your brain to stop producing essential hormones. This destroys your body's natural rhythm and ability to function normally. Think about it, Jessica, ten years is a long time."

Over the years I'd heard conflicting information about the birth control pills. Gynecologists swore by them, while most alternative practitioners felt they were synonymous with poison, since the pill was a synthetic hormone. But I hadn't wanted to get pregnant, and condoms and diaphragms usually gave me bladder infections, so I stuck with the pill until 1994, when a doctor told me it might be causing the headaches. I stopped popping the little orange tablets, a ritual I'd done every morning for ten years, but it didn't help the head pains and my periods never returned. Absence of menses was another thing that caused great concern, not just for obvious reasons, but because for six years not getting my period was a daily reminder that something wasn't right, that I was damaged, defective. My mother believed it was a delayed outcome of my earlier eating disorder, and maybe it was, but in my heart I felt it was more complicated than that. So, when Ursula told me that all of my major glands were inactive, and that this was a direct result of taking birth control pills, I just started to cry—not so much out of sadness, though that feeling was there, but more because the information fit.

"Do you think it's any accident that in places where the birth control pill is most often prescribed, the United States and Europe, the percentage of women who suffer from irregular menstruation and infertility is the highest in the world?" she asked.

"Is that true?" I said. "I had no idea."

"You might want to do some research," she said, a tinge of exasperation in her voice.

Her diagnosis had also revealed an infection in my left kidney and my bladder, my ovaries were not functioning properly, and I was anemic. As overwhelmed as I was, I was also relieved to have some answers.

"Except for the anemia, why didn't any of this show up on

the blood panels I've done over the years?" I asked.

"I look at the system from an energetic perspective," she said. "Sometimes I uncover problems that haven't shown up yet in blood work or X-rays. This is why the scientific community has some difficulty with my system. Not that my findings can't be measured, but often, they can only be measured by vibration. There are only a few people who have the ability to sense activity or disease on this level."

"What about the machine?" I asked. I had nothing to lose. I'd exhausted all my options in the States, in fact I'd begun to befriend my headaches, no longer desperately seeking a cure. But I was here to practice opening up, to do some things I would not have otherwise done.

"The machine will help, but you'll also need to take some supplemental medicines. You might want to come twice a week."

I knew that nothing would keep me away from this woman now. "How much will it cost?" I asked.

"About thirty US dollars per visit, including time on the machine and all the medicine. If you can't afford it, we can arrange a payment plan."

"Thirty dollars is fine," I said, aware that comparable treatment in the States would cost ten times that.

I felt I was on my way.

Twice a week, I traveled two hours by bus from the mountains to the city to be hooked up to Ursula's machine. Over time she started to warm up to me; her eyes seemed a little more animated and she even hugged me occasionally. "How was the ride?" she'd ask. We had a little joke about how long it took to get to her house from Antigua by "chicken bus" (the villagers used the local buses to transport their wares, which often included chickens). "An hour and forty-five minutes," I'd say, which meant it was a good day. Then she would lead me to the back room of her tiny apartment, where Mercedes would take over while Ursula attended to a living room full of patients. She treated at least twenty people a day, and Mercedes told me that several well-known doctors in Guatemala came to Ursula secretly for treatment.

I tried to schedule my appointments right before her lunch break, and more often than not we would end up talking for much of that time. One day, after several weeks of treatment, Ursula finished with her last patient and came back to ask me about my headaches.

"They're better," I said. "But it's hard to tell if it's because of my work with Joselo, or the machine and the medicine."

"Maybe it's both," she said. "Both polarities are needed to make up a balanced human being.

"Life is a delicate balance between two opposite poles," she continued, "the positive and the negative, the yin and the yang, the spiritual and the material. Nothing in the universe can exist without these polarities. The earth has two poles just like the body, and everything in nature. The fact that our world is in such bad shape indicates that we've lost our balance."

"How can we regain it?" I asked. Ursula's assistant reset the machine for my next frequency.

"Prayer is one effective way to bring the body of the universe back into balance, not to be rid of the material world, but to balance it out with the spiritual. Similarly, if we only concern ourselves with the spiritual realm and forget to attend to the material, we'd fly right out of this world."

I thought of Jesus' words: "We live in this world, but are not of it."

"Do you consider yourself to be a spiritual person?" I asked.

"I try to find a balance between the two polarities," Ursula said. "I believe a person is a lot like a tree: we need to be firmly rooted in the ground, with our arms stretched out to the heavens. The events of my life have led me to believe that there is a divine order to this universe."

I finished on the machine and Ursula invited me into her little yellow kitchen, where she served up two big bowls of homemade stew. I lit a fire and we settled in for a long lunch. Sheets of rain pounded the earth outside her picture window, and much to my surprise, she began to tell me her story.

"I was nineteen when the war broke out in Germany. It was 1939 and I was living with my family in the south, which was occupied by the Americans, but we weren't any safer for it. Death was all around me. I'm not Jewish, but many of my friends were, and I watched as several of them were murdered. I don't like to talk about that time, it was terrible. I did get married and have two children, but I remained dead inside." Ursula fell silent for a few seconds. Here was the sadness I'd sensed.

"After the war I left my husband. I wasn't in love with him. I spent the next ten years devoted to my work as a fashion designer, and I became pretty successful for a woman. But I was lonely and when in 1958 another man asked me to marry him, I said yes again, even though I wasn't in love. Don't marry unless you're in love."

I nodded, thinking about my ex-fiancé. I missed him.

"My second husband-to-be worked for Siemens Corporation. They were transferring him to another country, we didn't know where, but I didn't mind the idea of leaving Germany. In fact I wanted to leave. The company agreed to pay my way if we agreed to stay married for two years. I guess they'd had problems with couples who'd use the company to relocate and then split up, which is exactly what we'd end up doing, but I didn't know that at the time. The hardest part was saying goodbye to my children. They were grown up and wanted to stay in Europe, but still it was hard."

Ursula now seemed more eager to tell her story.

"My fiancé went ahead to get settled in his new territory," she went on. "I had to sell my business and close everything down first. But one week before I was scheduled to leave, I received a telegram from him telling me not to come, he didn't want to marry me after all. Some nerve he had. That man didn't know who he was dealing with. I didn't answer his telegram. I got on that plane and came to Guatemala."

"Was he here when you landed? Did he abandon you?" I asked.

"He was waiting at the gate, not too happy to see me, but he was there, all right. We agreed to strike a deal: we'd stay married for two years and then divorce, which suited me fine. Remember, I wasn't in love with him. Three months later he was transferred to El Salvador. I stayed here and we hardly saw each other after that."

"What did you do?" I asked.

"Well, I met some influential people at the German Embassy and started doing fashion design. I also met Henry, a German man who was seventeen years older than me. The first night I met him I understood why I agreed to marry my second husband, why I'd been willing to leave my children and my career in Germany, and I why I'd insisted on getting on that plane. I was coming to find Henry."

Ursula looked toward the photograph of Henry in a white laboratory coat.

"A doctor?" I asked.

"Yes, he was the first doctor in our family," she said. "He treated hundreds of people over the years—reflexology, chiropractic, and herbal remedies."

"When did you become a doctor?" I asked.

"Technically, not until after he died," she said, "but I started to diagnose his patients long before that."

I was confused.

"Two years after I arrived in Guatemala," she continued, "I suffered complications during a routine surgery and was pronounced clinically dead. It was the strangest experience of my life. I can't tell you what happened during those few minutes, it's just a blank space, but when I started breathing again, I knew something was different. I must have touched another realm. It was as if I'd acquired a new level of knowledge. Of course I didn't know it at the time, I was just grateful to be alive, but I knew something was different."

This sort of thing fascinated me. There was a time I teetered on having an obsession with near-death experiences and the nature of life after death. I'd always been enthralled by people's personal accounts of what happened in that space between life and death. Maybe I thought there were answers in that space, that somehow it could bring me closer to the truth, though after my recent encounter in the Osa I wasn't quite sure.

"A few years after my near-death encounter, I started to become very sensitive, not just emotionally, but psychically, which wasn't like me. I started to pick up strange things, vibrations and energy fluctuations, and at some point I was able to detect the location of water underground and radiation in the atmosphere. I say it now like it's normal, but it scared me half

to death. Of course I came to accept it. I guess I knew it was
related to my dying, which gave it a context, as crazy as it was,
and eventually word got around. Individuals and companies
started calling on me to help them. That's when I started diagnosing in healthcare; I wanted to see if I could apply the same
principles to help people. It worked."

Ursula glanced back to the picture. The way her eyes glazed
over and her skin paled told me that her pain was still very real.
"When Henry died, I felt like I'd lost a part of myself. We'd been
together for twenty-eight years and it was like losing a limb." She
lowered her voice. "We never actually married, though. Henry's
wife wouldn't give him a divorce, but we lived together as husband and wife for all those years, in the eyes of God, anyway.
I helped with his patients, diagnosing behind the scenes, but I
gave him all the credit. It's funny, with everyone else I needed
to be right, but not with him. I didn't care that I lived in his
shadow, I wanted him to get all the praise. But when he died—I
was seventy-three—I decided to go back to school and earn my
degree in natural medicine. It seemed like the right thing to do.
About five years later one of Henry's former patients gave me
the Bio Active Frequency Instrument. Now a lot of folks come
to see me, I'm glad I can help."

I was in awe of what Ursula had been through during her
eighty years: the anguish of war, the gift of love, the mystery of
death, a well-rounded life.

As for Ursula's diagnoses, there was still one point that confused me. When Ursula made a diagnosis, she took out that
old piece of paper with the numbers one to one hundred fifty
written in columns across the page. She had told me that each
number represented a certain disease and corresponded with a
specific frequency.

"How did you come up with a hundred fifty different frequencies and how did you determine which number correlated with which disease?" I asked.

Ursula's eyes widened a little and she peeked around the corner to make sure nobody was listening. "That's the most mysterious part of the story," she whispered. "It came to me in a dream one night, after I'd been praying for greater understanding of my gift. I had a vision of a man, a little wizard person, I think he even wore a cape. He came to visit me and some other people; he kept walking around like he was trying to determine something very important. Somehow I knew, I don't remember how, but I did, that whomever this man kissed on the forehead would be infused with a higher knowing. He kissed me.

"Then one day when I was reading the Bible something clicked. I knew that there were a total of a hundred fifty frequencies that corresponded with the hundred fifty psalms in the Bible."

Strangely, I believed her. Ursula wasn't the type to make this up.

"After I read over and meditated on the psalms," she continued, "I discovered that each one held a slightly different vibratory quality. I also figured out that each disease or grouping of diseases had a unique vibration, that no two were alike. I studied and researched and spent most of my waking hours contemplating this puzzle, and one day it all came together. I saw that the vibration of each diseased cell structure responded to one of the psalm vibrations."

"Have you ever been revisited by the man from your dream?"

"No," she said. "But I know I was chosen."

Ursula pulled a piece of paper from her desk drawer. "This passage in the Bible, John 9, verses one to three, speaks to me."

And as Jesus passed by, he saw a man blind from birth and his disciples asked him, "Rabbi, who sinned, this man or his parents, that he was born blind?" And Jesus answered, "Neither this man nor his parents sinned, but this happened so that the work of God might be displayed in his life."

"What does it mean to you?" I asked.

"I think that some people must endure sickness in order to make visible the work of God," she said. "And I believe that you are one of these people."

Ursula's words caught me off guard, but Joselo had told me something similar at our first meeting. "Do not forget, you are here to make good the work of Spirit. If you do not listen to your destiny, your health will continue poorly."

No doubt I had endured my share of suffering, just like everybody. The difference was that I had decided to dedicate my life to finding freedom from suffering, to forge a different relationship with it. I recalled the message from my vision at Hacienda Del Sol: "God is the energetic frequency of love. You must know this, live this, and share this. That is all."

Tears were streaming down my face. My journey was revealing its own unique story, and I was merely a spectator, along with everyone else.

THE DARK NIGHT

The Gita's subject is the war within, the struggle for self-mastery that every human being must wage if he or she is to emerge from life victoriously.

— *The Bhagavad Gita*

Chapter 13

DISCERNMENT

I sat quietly, basking in the warm July sun. The sky was crystalline blue, the lake glistened in the distance, and the air was still. I had been studying with Joselo for three months and today would be my first level of initiation: I would receive my pixom' kakol, or sacred bundle, and with it a new level of authority. Joselo stood behind my chair, accompanied by a small circle of priests, all of whom would assist in the ceremony. There was one other woman priest, the rest were men.

"Heart of heaven, heart of earth, heart of air, and heart of water," Joselo began, calling in the energies of the day and honoring the divinity of Maximón. "Today Jun Q'anil will receive spiritual husband, pixom' kakol, and begin rite of passage as Mayan priest."

I looked up toward the heavens and into Joselo's eyes. This moment held the sanctity of marriage, and like a nervous bride, I looked to my minister for reassurance. Joselo smiled down benevolently. "This bag is for healing," he whispered. "You must carry to all ceremonies and rituals, it contains the sacred red beans."

Somebody behind me lit the incense and began to pass it over everyone in the group to cleanse the energy field. The priests chanted and prayed and lit lots of candles, and eventually each one took a turn standing behind me, their strong hands resting heavily on my shoulders, sending out a prayer for my journey on the Camino. I felt vaguely uncomfortable with the whole arrangement, but endured it nonetheless. Was this how a bride felt right before she married the wrong man? I brought my attention back to the ceremony, upset that such a thought had entered my consciousness at such a sacred moment.

After the ceremony, it was customary to partake in a meal prepared and served by the initiate herself. Owing to my culinary ineptitude, I brought bagels and cream cheese (there was actually a small deli in Antigua), fresh baked banana bread, and lots of wonderful fruit: papayas, mangos, pineapple, watermelon. I pretended not to notice everyone's disappointment. Traditionally a shaman or priest is paid for his services by a typical homemade feast, often lasting for hours as the priests will eat until they can hardly move. It is for this reason that many Mayan medicine men are overweight, as it would be impolite of them not to receive "payment" for services rendered.

Despite the food shortage, we managed to have a good time, laughing and singing, lounging around on a sunny summer afternoon high in the mountains above Lake Atitlán. I lay down on the earth on my back, inhaling the sweet smell of grass and fresh soil as I stared up into space. Was this truly my destiny? It was hard to imagine that this was how the story might end, with me as a Mayan priest. I overheard Joselo speak my name and then he and another priest named Roberto began talking quietly.

I'd met Roberto at a previous fire ceremony, but hadn't paid much attention to him. Roberto was by no means a handsome man, with his bulbous nose and scars that looked like knife wounds splattered across his face. He looked weathered, worn. Like Joselo, Roberto was native to Guatemala, coming from a long line of Mayan priests, but unlike Joselo, who was a wise elder in his community, Roberto seemed less experienced. Where Joselo showed unshakable equanimity, Roberto seemed reactionary, and where Joselo was without ego, Roberto seemed to have something to prove. Roberto was, however, notorious for his ability to read the sacred red beans, and after a short exchange, Joselo announced that Roberto would instruct me in this practice. It seemed odd that I would be handed over to another priest, but I trusted my teacher. I remained on the grass for a while, waiting to see what would happen.

When it was time to start the ritual, I sat on the ground, opposite Roberto. He lit a few candles and said a blessing. Then he chose a flat surface on the earth and, spreading open a small hand-woven cloth, emptied out the contents of my pixom' kakol bag, revealing many little treasures. I carefully examined each item and inquired about its healing properties.

"What's this for?" I asked, picking up a miniature carving of an owl.

"Each item has special purpose," Joselo said. "Over time I teach you everything. But today, you learn only how to read red beans."

Like a fortune teller uses a crystal ball, or a psychic uses tarot cards, the Mayans use red beans for divination or to "read" a situation. Roberto told me that these beans came from red bean trees that were scattered about the country and were used for many purposes. So, in addition to egg ceremonies and fire rituals, I was about to learn the secret of this ancient tradition.

Roberto asked me to pose a question for a demonstration. "There is a book I want to write," I said. "Will it ever be published?"

He collected a small handful of beans and threw them like dice on his little green and blue cloth. He scanned the formation in which they had landed and he directed all of his attention on the red beans.

After a few minutes he spoke. "You will publish book one day, but there will be obstacles. A man who has power in publishing world will help you. His belief in you and your book will allow others to take notice. This is what I see."

"How do you see this?" I asked.

Roberto began to explain the subtleties of the red beans. "The beans will talk to you. First, you must practice to 'see'—formations, striations, different colors and sizes. Next you must call to intuition, most critical part. Look and tell me what you see."

I had learned from Sanda how to shift my gaze when tuning in to energy, so I could access information on the subtler levels. She had shown me that when I stared at an object for a long time, eventually my vision would begin to blur until the object's physical boundaries would soften or even fluctuate. Sometimes I had heard this referred to as "seeing double," and I decided to try this technique with the red beans.

Blocking out all distractions, I focused my attention on the bean configuration. It took a moment, but soon I was able to look past the beans themselves and see into their energetic field. Suddenly, one bean seemed to pop out. Intuitively I knew this represented me. Another bean was clearly the book, and still another seemed to suggest a third factor—the supposed man in power. There were also several beans clustered between "me" and the "book," as if signifying some sort of barricade or detour. I relayed what I saw to Roberto.

"Good," he said. "How you know this?"

"Just a gut feeling," I said.

"Maybe you a natural," he said. He smiled broadly and gave Joselo a slight nod. "Now I ask you question." He looked at me in a strange way, almost too closely, and I began to feel uncomfortable. I crossed my arms over my chest and waited.

"I want to know when will I marry?" he said.

I exhaled, relieved to know there was a woman in his life. I'd been feeling like he had his sights set on me. Thankfully, he had a girlfriend. I took my time to say the opening Quiché prayer, surprised at how naturally it rolled off my tongue. Joselo smiled proudly. Then I reached into my bag, delicately fingering the treasures hidden inside. I chose a few stray beans and shook them in my hand before tossing them onto the cloth, setting my intention to see clearly and objectively.

The first thing I noticed was that "her" bean was facing away from "his" bean, and that she was lighter in color. "Does this woman know you're interested?" I asked.

Roberto nodded yes.

"Because it looks like she's facing away from you," I continued.

Roberto didn't look happy with my interpretation, but nodded for me to go on. "Are you in contact with her?" I asked.

"Contact?"

"Do you talk to her?"

"Yes, we have spoke," he said.

I studied the beans for a few more moments.

"Does it look like we will go together?" he asked again, a little impatiently this time.

I felt smothered, as if energetic tentacles were creeping toward me. It had to be my imagination. I took a deep breath, pushed the feeling away and looked deeper into the beans. They were situated far apart with lots of "obstacles" in between. The prognosis for his intended relationship did not look hopeful, but I needed to be diplomatic. As a newcomer to this world, I didn't want to alienate anybody, least of all a pride-filled priest with war wounds covering his face. "What do I know about these red beans?" I said with a silly smile.

A muffled snicker ran through the group. I glanced over at Joselo, who looked uneasy. Roberto asked several more questions about his mystery woman, all of which I unknowingly answered correctly. As I determined that the woman was substantially younger, lighter skinned, and on a different life path than he, I had the increasing sense that he was guiding this line of questioning in my direction. I rejected the feeling. That would constitute a breach in ethics and integrity, both by Roberto as well as by my own teacher, but I couldn't shake the feeling that he was asking about me. I sighed loudly and rolled my eyes, indicating to Joselo that I was finished. But I couldn't seem to disengage from this lesson.

Joselo spoke up. "Enough practice for today," he said more to Roberto than to me. "She did good, no?"

I did not appreciate being talked about like I wasn't there. Maybe it was cultural for Mayan men to discuss women this way, or maybe I was being overly sensitive, but I didn't like it. I tried to hide my irritation as I collected my beans, placed them safely into their bag, and stored the whole bundle in my backpack.

"How about dessert?" I suggested, trying to change the subject. A delicious-looking chocolate cake made by Joselo's wife for the occasion was beginning to melt in the heat of the sun. I didn't know about anybody else, but I couldn't think of a better way to end this gathering. We completed the day with more ritual and song, and I was relieved to be finished with Roberto, when he approached me with several small gifts: a handmade bag, a special cloth for my red bean readings, and a bundle of wildflowers. My suspicions were confirmed. Under the guise of teacher, Roberto had been asking his questions about me. Wasn't that inappropriate? Even more, it seemed irreverent.

I suppose it was only a minor infraction; he was just acting like an adolescent boy testing the waters with his new crush, but the fact that he was a priest and assuming the role of teacher really bothered me. I knew that sexual misconduct happened among gurus and disciples. I had heard about spiritual teachers using their authority to manipulate naïve seekers, often enticing the student to engage in sexual relations. I wondered if that was the case with Roberto. Apparently, the Mayan world was no different than any other, and it had been naïve of me to foster the illusion that all teachers had integrity, like Sanda and Joselo. Now I had to face the truth that the reputation of many men in Central America as infamous womanizers could also include Mayan priests.

The next day, when Joselo and I had a moment alone, I asked him what he thought about the fact that Roberto was making a play for me during my initiation.

"The world is full of tricksters," he said. "Spiritual realm no different. We must all take care. But Roberto's questions were innocent, he meant no harm."

"Maybe," I said, "but Roberto has lost his credibility with me. Either he can be a teacher or he can pursue me romantically, but the two together feels very messy." I didn't add that I was disappointed in Joselo as well, that I thought he should have protected me, but Joselo always seemed able to read my mind.

He chuckled. "I knew his interest, yes, but he had to go in his own way. It served as good lesson, no?"

"It was humiliating," I said. "Everyone knew except me."

"But you did know," he insisted. "You knew something no

right from beginning. I saw. You need trust yourself. Yes, it's good to trust teacher, but more important you need trust yourself, listen inside. Use what happened at ceremony as opportunity to grow. See where you can stand more in your power."

"But I didn't want to go against your authority," I said, "especially in front of your community."

"Sometimes that's okay," he said gently. "Each meeting serves as lesson, sometimes help us move forward, sometimes no. You choose."

I thought about what he said. It was true that I had blindly trusted Roberto, choosing to ignore my intuition out of respect to Joselo. But now it was clear that if I didn't show myself the same respect, which meant honoring my inner wisdom no matter what was at stake, I would never fully embody my potential. I wasn't happy about the way things had transpired, but the lesson that accompanied that incident would be the initiator of change. Whether I was working with Joselo, Sanda, or Ursula, I had to learn to trust the teacher inside myself.

Chapter 14

DISILLUSIONED

I knew it was a bad omen the day my bus got stopped by the police. Riding the buses in Guatemala was a community experience, and over the months I had gradually taken a liking to it. I appreciated the ritual of coming together, Guatemalans and foreigners alike, forced to find common ground in such close quarters, despite our differences. I made it a habit on each ride to pay for my entire row, usually six people across, which served as a much-needed icebreaker. Generally, the gesture was met with cautious smiles and a few waves, as we'd try to communicate through a variety of languages. I was always struck by how many more similarities there were than differences—insecurities, fears, the tendency to keep separate in spite of the desire to connect.

On this particular day, though, I wasn't in the mood for socializing. I felt solitary, depressed, confused about my path. No longer sure of what I was doing, I was headed into the city to see Ursula, when the bus pulled over to the side of the road. I looked out the window to see the crisp military uniforms of officers who stood erect, their rifles in ready position. It wasn't uncommon for buses to be randomly stopped by the police, but it was never welcome, as the officers had the reputation of hassling young tourists. I had even heard stories about tourists being captured by the military, robbed, raped, and never seen again.

Being the only gringo on the bus, I wasn't surprised when the officer who came aboard looked directly at me. "Pasaporte," he said.

I didn't have it. I knew that I should always carry identification when I traveled around the country, but the odds of being robbed were higher than the odds of being stopped by the police. Who wanted to deal with replacing a stolen passport? My mind did somersaults, trying to figure a way out of this predicament, when the officer asked me to get off the bus. I knew this wasn't good.

I got off the bus and heard the coarse sand crunch beneath the officer's boots as he stepped away to consult with his superior. I prayed silently while the two men engaged in a short conversation about what to do with the girl with no papers. I began to feel nauseated. An incident with the police was the last thing I needed.

"We need take you in," the first officer said.

"But my passport's in Antigua, I'm just not carrying it," I said in perfect Spanish. "I'd like to call the U.S. embassy to inquire about my rights. This doesn't seem reasonable."

Visibly annoyed, the officer again consulted with his supervisor. I looked up at the bus, a sea of curious spectators peered back at me. Why didn't someone come to my rescue? I thought back to the red bean incident and how I had hoped Joselo would come to my aid. It was up to me, so I had to stay grounded and alert.

"Okay, señorita." The officer was back. He motioned for me to follow and waved the bus on. I stepped aside as dark diesel fumes clouded the atmosphere, holding my breath until the smoke dissolved, wishing the rest of my problems would melt away too. No such luck. There I was, alone with four military officers on the side of the highway in the mountains of Guatemala. I had no identification, no money, and no idea how to disentangle myself from this mess. I watched the bus slowly make its way up the mountain pass, with several pairs of eyes still staring at me from the back window.

We must have trekked two miles before arriving at the midway station, a dingy little mountain hut. The room was almost bare, except for four chairs and a table with a half-full bottle of whiskey on it. The cold, damp air had a foul odor; I wasn't sure if the smell originated from burnt garbage or if one of the officers had really bad body odor. The men stacked their firearms in a corner of the hut and sat. There was a phone, but it didn't appear they had any inclination to let me call the embassy.

"You stay here. Later we move you to police headquarters," one of them said in stilted English, his eyes roaming from me to the whiskey bottle and back to me again.

Already I felt like a prisoner. I tried not to think about what might come next, but my mind had shifted into overdrive, frantically working out a plan for escape.

"Can I call my friend?" I asked. "She's expecting me for lunch."

They eyed one another.

"Who your friend?" one of them asked.

I shifted nervously. "She's the wife of the German diplomat—I'd hate for her to get worried and come looking for me." I wasn't sure where I was going with this, but I waited for their reaction. I buried my hands in my back pockets and felt a folded bill. I'd forgotten that I'd slipped 500 quetzals, the equivalent of forty U.S. dollars, into my pocket that morning to pay Ursula. "Here," I said, handing the money to the head honcho. "This should cover the phone call. And if it isn't enough, when my friend gets here, I know she'll add something extra to it."

He seemed satisfied. He took the money, pocketed it, and grunted toward the phone. Now, if I could just remember Ursula's telephone number. I conjured a mental picture of my address book where I had written it down. I'd had some luck with this technique in college and graduate school, using a photograph in my mind to recall information. Sometimes I could pull up a screen and retrieve it all, other times only portions of what I needed. It had saved me on many exams, and now I hoped it would save me from a lot worse.

By some miracle I saw it, the phone number that is still etched in my mind today. I exhaled and picked up the phone. The sound of the dial tone made me feel better, reconnecting me with the outside world. I dialed her number, banking on the probability that these men didn't understand much English.

"Buenos?" Ursula's assistant said on the other end of the phone.

"It's Jessica," I said. "I'm in trouble. Please put Ursula on the phone."

"What's wrong?" she asked.

"I'm with the police."

She put me on hold and I smiled at the men who were leering at me.

I waited what felt like a long time. "Yes?" Ursula said finally.

"Ursula," I said, holding back tears. "It's Jessica. I need your help. The police have me in custody for not carrying my passport. I'm alone in the mountains and I don't feel safe." I gave her my approximate location and asked her to bring money.

"My driver's on his way," she responded.

"Please hurry."

"You'll be okay," she said. "I'll see you soon." The line went dead.

One hour and another bottle of whiskey later, the officers were showing signs of impatience. Their gazes seemed to linger longer as they passed the bottle around. One man actually started to drool, tiny opaque bubbles forming at the corners of his mouth. Normally, I didn't break a sweat even on a hot day, but now, standing by the door in this freezing cold hut, my entire shirt was wet with perspiration. I was entertaining the idea of making a run for it, since I was sober and they weren't, when Ursula arrived with her driver. I saw her silhouette behind the tinted back window and it took a lot of concentration not to fall apart right then. The driver got out of the car with several sacks full of food, as if preparing to serve lunch, while Ursula emerged from the back seat, apologizing profusely to the officers for my having inconvenienced their day.

"She's a visiting language student under our supervision." She nodded in my direction. "I'm terribly sorry for any trouble. We'll make sure she carries her papers from now on."

I was fascinated by how she was handling the situation.

Her driver began to serve up a very civilized lunch, and much

to my dismay, I had to share a meal with these men who stunk
of alcohol. They tore into the food and continued with their
whiskey, periodically smiling in Ursula's direction. About twenty
minutes into the meal, Ursula announced that she had to get
back to her patients. Without missing a beat, she handed the
head officer the equivalent of 200 dollars and motioned to me
to get ready to leave. We shook hands all around, smiles were
exchanged, and before I knew it, I was free and we were driving
away, as if this had been a normal lunch.

Gratefully, we sat in silence for some time. I guess Ursula
knew I was still spooked, and her driver expertly followed
the sharp mountain curves, which felt strangely reassuring. "You
were lucky," she said finally.
    "I know. Thanks for coming."
    "I hope you've learned a lesson. You can't get too comfort-
able here, Jessica. You're not in the United States and the rules
are different."
    "I know. I've been learning things the hard way lately." I told
her about the incident up at the lake with Roberto and Joselo.
"It's disillusioning when people and situations aren't what they
seem."
    "Yes," she agreed, "but things are rarely as they appear, because
we tend to interpret events based on our perception. The problem is that our perception is often clouded, incomplete, and we
go through life thinking that's all there is. But when we become
dis-illusioned, we are forced to see things more clearly, more
as they really are."
    What Ursula said was true. These experiences had shattered
some powerful illusions—illusions of safety, security, the integ-

rity of others—and in their wake I would be forced to see things differently.

We rode in silence as the rain splattered the windshield.

"So much of my life has been based on illusion," I said. "Seeing what I want to see, looking for validation from others."

She nodded.

"I've spent so much time searching for peace, trying to disengage from these false patterns, and I think I've changed a lot. I guess I thought this journey would bring clarity to everything in my life, that it would be the culmination of all my work. But the truth is, I'm more confused than ever. I feel isolated and I really don't know what I'm doing here."

"I'm glad to hear you say that," Ursula said.

"Why? It feels terrible."

"Because when we truly realize that we don't know, the real transformation can begin. I've wondered if your decision to walk the Camino came out of fear rather than a genuine calling."

There was truth in what she said. I knew that, but so far I hadn't been able to admit it to myself.

"Becoming a Mayan priest may fit the image of what you thought should happen on your journey," she said, "but in your heart does it ring true for you?"

I'd been wrestling with this question for months. Achieving the rank of a Mayan priest would allow me to come away from this journey with something tangible, something concrete, but I was no longer sure that it was congruent with who I was. If I wasn't being true to myself, I'd be worse off than when I started. Would the whole trip end up being for nothing?

"Life rarely looks how we think it should," Ursula said, "but still we hold on to our illusions, clinging to false security, no matter how unhappy we are. And then, when we get wise to what we're doing, we may make some changes, but the ego is very cunning and just conjures up more sophisticated illusions. It's a vicious cycle, but eventually the whole structure has to crumble because it's not real."

Had I constructed another illusion about becoming a Mayan priest, simply replacing one false identity with another? I feared I had. But if I wasn't meant to walk the Camino, why had I been led to Guatemala and to Joselo? I leaned my head back and closed my eyes. I knew what I was leaving behind, but where was I headed? After all this time, all the ceremonies and decision making, I still had no answers. I only knew I was terrified of facing myself once again, of being a woman on her own with no real identity. If I decided to go against my decision to become a Mayan priest, I'd be thrown into the pain of disassembling my life yet again. I'd done that once in Los Angeles. It had been agonizing and disorienting and I just wasn't sure I could do it again.

Chapter 15

MADNESS

I walked down the familiar streets of Antigua, but nothing looked the same. I studied the cracks in the cobblestones through sheets of biting rain, feeling alone. When I got back indoors, I sat in my loft and watched the immense volcano belch giant smoke rings, looking for reasons to get out of bed. My simple routine—studying, eating, bathing, and relating with others—seemed utterly meaningless and required tremendous effort.

I ruminated about my life, my family and friends, my career, and my ex-fiancé, but I didn't feel much. Bits of memories and conversations circulated through my mind, but I was so disconnected, they seemed like somebody else's memories. I felt like an imposter, peering into what had once been my life, a life to which I now had no attachment or relationship whatsoever.

Feeling like a stranger in my own body concerned me deeply, but even worse was the fear that I would not be able to create a life for myself.

I had no motivation to travel to the lake or into the city, so I stayed close to home, hoping my depression would pass, fearing

that it wouldn't. Doña Della left soup and bread on my doorstep, which I hardly touched. Finally, after a week of fasting, I
forced myself to go to the market.

On the street, I counted the fissures in the sidewalk, reminding myself that I did indeed exist and there were cracks in the
earth to prove it. It was as if everything had fallen away—all
aspirations, motivations, methods, and teachers—and I was left
alone with myself. I had been alone before throughout this journey, but now I felt disconnected from the world.

After walking eight blocks, I entered the marketplace, picked
out some fruits and vegetables, and then a strange thing happened. The images before me began to fade in and out, merging
with the existing scenery, overlapping to form a matrix or grid. I
closed my eyes, slowed my breathing, and tried to stay grounded.
The only time I had experienced anything like this was during
meditation or before falling asleep, that in-between state of consciousness when strange fragments and images flashed before
me, but this was my first full-blown waking episode.

I closed my eyes and opened them. For a moment, everything
appeared normal, so I continued shopping. I reached into my
purse to pay for some apples, but when I collected my change
from the vendor, I couldn't remember where I was or how to
count the currency. I faltered, unsure whether to giggle or cry,
but within seconds I plunged into a deep, echoing laughter. The
vender glanced at me, her eyes moved from side to side as if
trying to assess the situation, and then she handed me the bag
of fruit. I stumbled over to a corner and tried to collect myself,
but I only became further disoriented, alternating between short
cries and laughter about nothing in particular. I wondered if I
were going insane.

Suddenly, a woman moved toward me. With each step, her
form metamorphosed, reconfiguring until I could no longer see

her skin or her facial features. Ancient archetypal images were superimposed over her face: The Princess, The Warrior, and The Evil Witch all came alive, teasing and mocking me, before melting away to reveal nothing but a bare skull. I inhaled sharply, quickly looked away from her, and scanned the crowd. Had anyone else seen this? Apparently not. They were all going about their business as usual. The woman passed by me and smiled a toothless grin. I began to weep like a newborn babe, completely unrestrained, devastated by my own lack of control.

I needed to get back home, quickly. On the way, I saw a vision of Joselo, his calm disposition, his reassuring smile. He told me to relax, not to worry, that everything would be okay. I saw Ursula also, reminding me that I was overdue for my treatment. When I looked past the images, the grid was there again, behind the scene before me. Terrified that I had lost my mind, I picked up my pace. Was I about to disappear too?

Ducking inside the loft, I dead-bolted the front door and slid to the floor, panting for breath. For an instant I felt safe, temporarily forgetting that the images had arisen from within me. I wasn't any safer indoors than on the street. I reminded myself to breathe. I was certain about only one thing: everything I knew or thought to be real was irreparably falling apart. It wasn't only relationships and priorities. Now I questioned reality itself. I needed to talk to Sanda.

I knocked on Doña Della's door and asked to borrow her cordless phone. She handed it to me and I hurried outside, finding a little spot in the garden to make my call. It was a spectacular fall day, the foliage lush from months of rain, the air crisp and sweet, but I was too distracted to absorb any of it. I started to dial Sanda's number and hesitated, feeling disappointed that I still needed guidance. But this wasn't the time to pretend otherwise. Sighing with resignation, I placed the international call, wondering how in the world to communicate what had just happened.

Sanda answered the phone herself. "Hello?"

"It's Jess," I said. "I'm in trouble."

"What's going on?"

I wiped away tears and did my best to explain the events. I described my meetings with Joselo and Ursula, and my decision to become a Mayan priest.

I told her how my doubts and confusion had led to feelings of disillusionment, and now isolation and depression. "I've lost my motivation to go on. I don't care about enlightenment, transformation, or anything else. I've lost the ability to see beauty. I can't appreciate a simple cup of tea or a kind word from a friend. I've touched realms I've only dreamed about, found teachers I've only read about, journeyed to places I've always fantasized about, and I can't enjoy any of it. It seems that while I was trying to find myself, I got more lost."

"Breathe, Jessica," she reminded me.

I inhaled.

"You've come upon a difficult and unavoidable part of this path," she said. "I'm not surprised."

"What are you talking about?"

She sighed. A cool breeze of relief washed over me as she spoke. She told me that when a person embarks on a journey like this, with the intention to become conscious, the whole universe conspires to make it happen. But it's never easy. All the fears become magnified and our courage gets tested again and again.

"The work you did before you left Los Angeles prepared you, but still you're being tested," she said. "It's part of the process, Jess, the brushes with death, the confusion, the intense aloneness. It creates a kind of madness. How could it be otherwise when everything you've known, everything you thought to be real, now seems so uncertain, so unreal? I know it's terrifying, but remember this is why you worked hard to develop a strong center before you took this journey. And now, you can't turn back. You must rise to the challenge and finish what you've started."

"I don't think I can," I muttered. "I can hardly get out of bed, make my own food, or even take a shower."

"Jessica," she said forcefully, "it's not time to call this off. You must dig deeper to find your strength. Do whatever it takes, talk to God, meditate, whatever is necessary to stay connected. But you can't allow your fear to take over."

I told her about the episode in the marketplace. "I know it sounds crazy, but I saw a woman's face transform into different mythical creatures. Then I had a vision of Joselo and Ursula talking to me." I stopped for a moment to breathe before whispering into the phone, "Sanda, I think I'm losing my mind."

"In a way, you are," she said. "It sounds like you're experiencing shamanic dismemberment. Didn't Joselo prepare you?"

I remembered Joselo had mentioned something about dismemberment once, briefly, but I didn't think it would actually happen. "What does shamanic dismemberment mean?" I asked.

"The intensity of your journey is forcing you to reconfigure your energy at the cellular level. This can only happen when the rational mind gets sufficiently worn down and can get out of the way. Your intellect can't fight anymore. That's why you feel depressed and hopeless.

"But now that your mind has let go, your energy body can begin to rebuild. It's like the matrix you saw in your vision. Jessica, you're not going crazy, but you are experiencing a kind of death. You're also being reborn as a more conscious and complete human being.

"You need to find a way to ground yourself during this process. You must use all the tools you've gathered to re-establish your connection."

"For God's sake Sanda, I watched people's faces disintegrate before my eyes. What the hell am I supposed to do with that?"

"Nothing," she said calmly. "It's part of the process. Just experience what's happening, but don't try to control it. You can't use reason when it comes to this stuff. The more you fight, the crazier you're going to feel. Remember, this journey is about strengthening your ability to trust. Try to let go a little, embrace your internal chaos, don't try to make sense of it."

I took a long, deep breath.

"You're all right," she said. "Your job now is just to be present, to stop searching for someone or something to rescue you, and to be awake in your experience, even when you're terrified. You must stand in the middle of the fire and remember who you are."

"Maybe I'm not cut out for this," I said.

"Oh, yes you are. Now, do you still have the stone I gave you?"

"Yes."

"Good, it's time to use it to get stronger. Every day at noon sit quietly, hold it, and focus. We'll connect up energetically. You must face your solitude, but remember you're not alone in this journey."

The line crackled. We were about to lose the connection. I didn't want her to go.

"One more thing," Sanda said.

I could barely hear her over the static. "Remember that chaos often precedes transformation. Hang in there, Jess. I believe in you."

We said goodbye.

I dropped the phone to the ground. If I could have returned to my safe familiar life in that instant, I would have, but the door had been shut, at least temporarily, and there was no turning back. I picked up the phone and stood. The debate was over. I had already made my choice, so I might as well face the inevitable truth that the only way out, was in.

Chapter 16

DISMEMBERMENT

I guess I shouldn't have been surprised when, two days after my conversation with Sanda, Joselo showed up at my door. I collapsed into his arms sobbing, my body shaking in his embrace. Despite my confusion, I knew I didn't want to become a Mayan priest.

"Tranquilo," Joselo said, trying to comfort me.

"I can't do it," I said. "I can't walk the Camino."

"That not so important, " he said. "What is important you find what you're looking, the truth. Teachers tell you many things, point you in many directions, but in the end you must see truth for yourself. Come, we must go to the mountains one last time."

"But a trip to the mountains feels dangerous right now," I said.

"Yes, your nervous system has stress, it is true. You go now through dismemberment."

He and Sanda were saying the same thing.

He went on. "Your mind is soft, you are moving through

layers very quickly. You must use as opportunity to travel in deeper. We will design special ritual, but right now, practice to surrender. Watch it unfold. Now, let us go."

I had no idea what Joselo had in mind, but I trusted him enough to collect a few things: jacket, jeans, umbrella, a few toiletries. Before we left, I scanned the small loft, wondering whether I'd ever return.

Joselo had rented a four-wheel-drive truck, and as soon as I climbed in we were speeding down the highway to God only knew where. The windows were down and the wind whipped through my hair while a woman sang a sad love song in Spanish on the radio. I had reached a breaking point; if I didn't move through this no-man's land I would risk getting stuck here. I didn't want that, so I tried to breathe and stay present, but soon noticed that Joselo wasn't heading to the lake. Rather, he drove to the opposite side of the country, through tropical jungle, where the air was thick with humidity and the smell of salt water. We were headed to the sea. Perhaps the change in climate would do me good.

Around noon Joselo pulled off the main highway and gestured for me to get out of the truck. He handed me what looked like a homemade map and a bag of supplies. "If you walk into jungle from here"—he pointed—"you find cave hidden deep in forest."

I looked at him. "What are you saying? Aren't you coming with me?"

"No, Jun Q'anil, you must go alone," he said softly.

"You're kidding, right?"

"Use jungle and all habitantes to guide you, and know that you are watched over."

The panic was back. "But I'll die out there, Joselo."

"It is possible, but no likely," he said. His eyes held a glow.

"I see you again soon."

I sat still for a moment, closing my eyes. I'd be mad to hike into the jungle. Maybe I should refuse. But then what? I had come this far, trusting the people and situations that had presented themselves. True, I stood on very shaky ground, yet I felt I had no choice but to push on. I remembered Sanda's stone that was tucked away in my pocket. A lifeline. I took it out, placing the rock firmly in my left hand. I looked toward the jungle and back at Joselo as I slowly pulled up the door handle and slid out of the truck. "What will I do when I find the cave?" I asked.

"You will know," he said. "Just be still."

I tiptoed down the narrow path leading into the forest, feeling like a little girl creeping around my bedroom at night. I was aware of every invisible crunch, swoosh, and tweet, stopping every few minutes to make sure that an ax murderer wasn't following me. I laughed at myself, and was glad that I could see the humor in my terror.

Then I heard a sound, a voice, maybe. I stopped to listen. It couldn't possibly be a human sound. Who else would be out here? I stood still, certain that I was about to be killed, when a family of ten Cakchiquel Indians appeared from around the bend. Our eyes locked. As frightened as I was by their presence, I was also relieved to see life out here. I'm sure they had no idea what to make of me. I forced a slight smile and said hello, hoping they spoke Spanish. "I'm looking for this cave," I said, pointing to a spot on my map. I wasn't sure why I told them this, but Joselo had told me to use the jungle and all of its inhabitants to guide me.

The males in the group stared me up and down.

This made me nervous. I decided to try to speak Quiché, hoping it might make them feel more friendly toward me. "The shaman, Joselo Carcamo, has sent me to find the cave. Do you know where it is?"

"Why you go there?" asked one of the women.

"Today is belejeb ajmaq," I said. "The day of forgiveness. I must perform a ceremony." That got their attention.

"You follow us," said the first man. "We show you way." Supposing that I had been elevated from strange white woman to friend, I relaxed a little. As I followed this family into the Guatemalan jungle, the trees became bigger, the birds sang louder, and the colors were much brighter than before. The children glanced back periodically from their hiking—it looked more like dancing and playing—to check on me. They examined my clothes, hair, and triple-story hiking boots, while they climbed barefoot through the forest. One boy looked like a little wizard, and when he smiled, his brilliance lit up the sky. I named him Niño Mágico (magical child) because he clearly carried a special kind of wizardry. He seemed to like the name, for he broke into a huge smile when I said it.

After walking steadily for about two hours, we reached a flat area that jutted out over the mountains. The view of the distant ocean was spectacular. At the edge of the bluff was a large cross representing the four cardinal points and marking the entrance to the holy land. We stopped to catch our breath and light our candles, showing deference to the spirits by asking permission to enter their domain. I had once found this ritual awkward, but now, as I bent down to kiss the earth, I found the familiarity of the process comforting. After all this time, it finally had become a part of me.

As we prepared to move ahead, the male elder in the group motioned to our right. There, erupting out of the earth stood two hundred-foot boulders. Where had those rocks come from? They hadn't been there five minutes ago. Or had they? Things started to look blurry and I prayed I wasn't about to have one of my meltdowns. Niño Mágico noticed my alarm and immediately came to my side. The elder man told me not to worry, that the rocks weren't visible until we received permission to enter. "It is good you travel with us," he said.

Scaling down a boulder would be difficult enough, but doing so while carrying bundles of heavy materials and supplies was another thing altogether. My companions, however, managed to tote their own sacks as well as mine, transforming themselves into a human rope that secured our hazardous descent. I was passed effortlessly from one serene face to another, as if this was their usual routine, while we all slowly lowered ourselves down from this mammoth rock.

When we arrived safely at the base of the ancient boulders, we all stopped to listen, as if these old rocks had a story to tell. No longer bound to the laws of time and space, I felt weightless as Niño Mágico and I scrambled down the remaining steep cliff side, so light, we hardly touched the ground. When we landed, I looked up to where we had begun our descent. How would I get back up? I pushed the thought out of my mind, deciding that it would happen however it happened—or it wouldn't. It was that simple.

When I turned to see what my guides would do next, the whole family had veered off to the left, blending into the background of the jungle. "Wait," I shouted. I felt like Alice in Wonderland calling after the White Rabbit who was fleeing with no explanation. I scanned the surrounding terrain for some movement or hint of color, but there was only deep stillness. I heard my own breathing, my heart beating. I feared I wouldn't find my way out. I looked at the map Joselo had given me. It showed the cave next to a waterfall, but otherwise the map was of little help. I looked in my bag and saw that I had enough food and water for three days.

I heard the falling water a moment before spotting the cave, deep at the bottom of a ravine. The day had become overcast, steel-gray clouds moved in from the horizon, threatening. Carefully, I made my way down the steep incline, putting one foot in front of the other, looking for footholds, grabbing onto vines and branches to keep from slipping. Covered in mud, I eventually reached the bottom.

Joselo had instructed me, when performing a ceremony, to light candles in each corner to determine a cave's depth. I knew that somewhere in these hidden caves were stone faces etched in the walls, depicting one or another of the Mayan gods. It was important to find these etchings and pay homage to them by kissing the wall and lighting candles all around. I cleared the area and put out my materials for the ceremony. Then I sat down and lit a small fire.

Now there was nothing left to do, so I sat, alone in a dark cave at the bottom of a ravine in the Guatemalan jungle. My mother would have dropped dead of a heart attack if she knew. I smiled to myself, realizing that finally I could stop running, since I had nowhere left to go, nobody to instruct me, no rituals to distract me. I closed my eyes, dropping into a deep inner space, and contemplated my ultimate question: If I wasn't a therapist, a Mayan priest, a sick person, a well person, a happy person, a confused person, or a person who was seeking enlightenment, who was I? What invisible force animated all these aspects of self, but in itself was none of these things? I would sit in this cave until I knew the answer.

There is a low buzzing noise in my ear. I open my eyes to find that the inside of the cave is a mass of bees, hundreds of them, flying in every direction. The low buzz becomes deafening as the bees crawl in and around my ears. I resist the temptation to swat them away as they circle madly over the fire, in and around the rocks and candles, and crawl all over me. Covered in bumblebees, I doubt very much that I will make it through this experience alive. I am barely breathing. I know that if stung I will die in this cave. The fire jumps well above four feet, causing the silhouettes of different creatures to dance against the far wall.

Imagining what it would feel like to be a bee myself, I remember that in the Mayan teachings the bee is the animal counterpart of ajmaq, the energy of forgiveness. Ajmaq also represents the mind in its ultimate state of illumination, or as Joselo says, "a cerebral lightning rod." Yet, I have no idea what to do with the information, so I remain still, alert.

My body begins to tingle. I look down at my legs and feet, and I am able to see these body parts in a detached way, as if they aren't mine. Gradually, the skin peels away and my legs begin to liquefy, revealing the underlying muscles and tendons. I can see veins pulsing with blood. Now I see bone, until this too begins to deteriorate, leaving only a slight residue of bone-colored ash. My upper torso, mid-torso, and finally my lower torso undergo the same meltdown. My entire body has evaporated while awareness remains intact.

I feel a powerful blast of lightning and I am gone, empty, nowhere and everywhere at the same time. I surrender into an ocean of laughter—there is only pure awareness, independent of form. I am part of a greater whole that has always been and always will be alive within me. In this extraordinary moment, everything that has come before makes sense—each person and event, all the turmoil and triumph, have brought me one step closer to this truth. There are no words that can touch this experience; a huge burden has been lifted. I am nothing, I am everything. I am free.

AWAKENING MIND

What you are looking for is what is looking.

— *St. Francis*

Chapter 17

THE DEATHLESS

Awakening completely relaxed, I looked down, half expecting not to see my legs, but they were both there, intact. What the hell had happened? A few bees were still buzzing around, the only living witnesses. The fire had gone out and time had passed. At first it was hard to move, as if I had been frozen in one place for many days. Eventually, my joints loosened up and I stretched out like a cat, growing and lengthening with each breath. My body felt light, and I luxuriated in the fullness of my stretch. In no hurry to get anywhere or do anything, I just stretched out contentedly in the interior of this dark, damp cave. Hunger called, so I scavenged the bag Joselo had provided and munched happily on a peanut butter and jelly sandwich. I gulped down an entire bottle of water, unconcerned by the overflow squirting from the corners of my mouth and onto my lap. I laughed heartily, like I had just heard a very funny joke.

"Who's laughing in there?" came a familiar voice from outside the cave.

I giggled like a child who delights in a game of hide-and-seek, aware that she has been found, even though the adult pretends not to see her.

"Who's there?" This time the voice was closer, and a grinning Joselo soon emerged from the darkness. He looked straight into my eyes and we exchanged a knowing smile; we didn't need words. I looked around the cave one last time while I gathered my things and recited a short blessing. I was filled with gratitude. Joselo and I made our way outside.

The hike out of the jungle was exhilarating; the vegetation was lush and a rainbow of wildflowers blanketed the hillside. I stopped to watch a fluorescent orange caterpillar inch its way across the trail; a woodpecker busily drilled into a nearby tree. The sunshine felt nourishing. A hawk circled above as Joselo and I walked through a sea of silver butterflies dancing along our path. The butterflies made me feel as if my guides were with me—Sanda, Zina, Chloë, Ursula—celebrating my emergence from the chrysalis. Inhaling the rich terracotta earth and sticky ocean air, it struck me that this was exactly what my journey was about, becoming free of all burdens so that I could see. It was astonishingly simple.

"So?" Joselo said eyeing me closely.

"My search is over," I announced. "I've spent many years waiting for lightning to strike, to receive a tiny drip of enlightenment, to find a special healer to heal me, when the truth has always been right in front of me."

"Sí," he said.

"All my efforts to escape my own suffering actually brought me full circle to meet it. When I finally stopped, when I decided to investigate the essence behind all of my *identities*, I was startled to find that what was there was just wide-open space. This space was alive, pulsing, like the stillness I've known in meditation, but this time I recognized the stillness as myself."

Joselo just smiled.

In that moment I realized that as long as I attached my desire or intention for truth onto a particular person or experience, freedom would always remain one step away. Until now, I had overlooked what was already perfect, whole, and complete. This wholeness—call it God, Awareness, Essence, Source—was simply who I was, who we all were, and it was always available, not just in meditation and altered mind states, but right then, right there. Joselo stood perfectly still, I could tell he was talking to the trees and the wind and the animals of the land. In that moment, I heard things I had never heard before, first the stillness and then the wisdom beyond it.

It was dark by the time we arrived back at the loft. My eyes filled with tears when I thought back to my first encounter with Joselo, his intangible and expansive Buddha-like presence. I understood now that this was the result of his living fully in each moment and not grasping for the next, whether he was climbing a mountain, performing a ceremony, or drinking a tall glass of Coke in some out-of-the-way village.

"Are you sure you're not the Buddha masquerading as a Mayan priest?" I said, wiping away my tears.

"We all meet in same place," he said, smiling. "You traveled through the layers, went to world of the deathless. You saw. You know."

Joselo had taught me many things, but the most important teaching was simply being in his presence and absorbing his essence. I was relieved to know that there was nothing I needed to do in order to become free, because freedom was my true nature, whether it took the form of a Mayan priest, a Buddhist monk, or nothing at all.

"Thank you," I said finally, aware that no words could convey my full gratitude. "And for introducing me to Ursula—she's remarkable."

"Yes, she is wise woman," he said. "Stubborn, but wise." And then he added: "You also wise woman. You are Jun Q'anil, very powerful force. You must use your magic carefully and for good."

I nodded.

"Life is big mystery," he said. "We do not know what will happen next. Stay alert, Jun Q'anil, may the spirit gods watch over you."

Joselo and I embraced. I felt an unexpected wave of relief that I would not be walking the Quiché way, trying to create an identity that wasn't authentic, but I vowed not to forget this man or the qualities he embodied, or the fact that he had helped deliver me back to myself.

"I only show you what is already there," he said, back to his mind-reading tricks. "Now go and be happy. And remember, freedom is right here, in color of sky, sound of wind, in deep stillness. No more and no less."

And then, just as mysteriously as he had once appeared, Joselo disappeared into the Guatemalan night.

Chapter 18

EQUANIMITY

Freed from the burden of making something happen, I enjoyed each remaining moment in Guatemala. I spent hours resting in the garden, eyes closed, face turned toward the sun, appreciating the perfection of just being. What could be more important than being awake and alive in this moment, or feeling that this moment was enough, just as it was? Nothing had outwardly changed in my life, I still had no particular identity, no possessions, and no special person with whom to share things. Yet I felt whole.

I returned to a daily yoga and sitting practice, watching the comings and goings of my mind. Now, I had increased compassion and curiosity, and no longer wished I was somewhere else, with someone else, or doing anything else. I felt present and free. Difficult thoughts and feelings still arose and would continue to, but my relationship with them had changed. After he had a stroke, Ram Dass, one of the foremost consciousness teachers in the West, said: "The hindrances of mind never stop coming, but they become like old friends; they hold less power;

they are more easily seen."

So too had I developed a wiser relationship with the work-
ings of my own mind.

For two months I wrote, slept, sat, and completed my course
of treatments with Ursula. I had gone from sixty minutes on her
machine twice a week to no treatments at all. The head pains had
diminished, my energy increased, and my overall health seemed
dramatically improved. But the most surprising change came at
midnight on my thirty-second birthday. I walked to the bathroom after a little party thrown by my local pals, and found I
had gotten my period. It was by far the greatest birthday present
of all: after several years, my internal balance had returned.

One day, on one of my trips into the city to see Ursula, she
announced that I was healed. "You're all better," she said. "I'm
giving you the green light to go home."

I had grown attached to this woman, taking refuge in her
home every week, rain or shine, for the past six months. Ursula
had provided a critical anchor for my journey, and I felt sad at
the thought of leaving her. "I can't be all better," I said, smiling.
"Now I won't have an excuse to come see you each week."

"You didn't need an excuse to visit me, but you are indeed
well."

"I can't believe it," I said. "Just when I'd let go of trying to
fix my health problems, I got dropped off in your living room.
You've restored my faith in miracles, Ursula."

"Life is amazing, isn't it?" she said. Then she looked at me
with an air of excitement. "And now, I have something I want
to give you."

She scurried back into the recesses of her apartment, her ballet
slippers scuffling along the wood floors. Maybe fairy godmothers
existed after all. I glanced around her living room, taking mental pictures of everything, knowing this might be the last time

I'd sit on her red vinyl couch or see the many diplomas on the walls. I bowed to the photograph of Henry, her late husband. He must have been a great man.

"Here it is," Ursula said, slowly lowering herself onto the couch. I could tell she was pleased about the gift; she practically had to sit on her hands to keep from opening it. I looked into her pale blue eyes. The sadness was still there, but it seemed to have lifted slightly, as if her own burdens had been lessened. Maybe she too had benefited from our time together. She patted my knee and shot me an endearing look, and then she couldn't hold back any longer; she delicately unfolded the white tissue paper to reveal a small pendant. It was the Star of David.

"It belonged to Henry," she was saying. "He wore it around his neck and hardly ever took it off. He said it held special significance and was very meaningful to him. Before he died he gave it to me, said it was time to pass it along. Now it's yours."

I couldn't speak; I just looked at the pendant.

"Do you remember the dream I told you about?" Ursula asked. "The one where the old man came and kissed me on the forehead?"

"Yes."

"There is one thing I didn't tell you about that dream: the man had the Star of David etched onto his forehead. When you told me about the vision you had at the house of Maximón, and your visit with the little boy, I knew you were the next person to wear this pendant." She clasped the necklace around my neck.

I touched it with my hand and got up. "I need to see something," I said. I walked over to the photograph of Henry and took a closer look. He was wearing an object around his neck that was partially hidden by his laboratory coat. "Is he wearing this pendant in the picture?" I asked.

Ursula nodded.

"Did he say where it came from?"

"He didn't say exactly, something about a survivor giving it to him after the war. But it doesn't matter, because I want you to have it."

"Thank you," I said.

"Wear it as I have," she continued, "as a reminder that the path chooses us, not the other way around."

"I think it's both," I said. "The path may choose us, but we also choose it. We have the power to make choices along the way."

"True," she said, smiling. "Very true."

Epilogue

REENTRY

My sneakers made a loud suction sound as I made my way through the brightly-lit corridors of Los Angeles International Airport. My big black suitcase was missing a wheel, so I dragged it as best I could while shouldering two gigantic duffel bags full of gifts and paraphernalia for family and friends. Travelers darted to and fro: men and women on cell phones, foreigners, families of various sizes. Some met my gaze, some didn't. I was straddling two worlds: part of me walked through the airport, preparing to hop in a taxi and slip back into the fold, another part still very much in Guatemala. I didn't know it at the time, but it would take a full three months before I was entirely back in Los Angeles.

Another strange phenomenon followed me around for those first three months. Athletes call it the zone, the sensation of being so completely absorbed in attention that any sense of self falls away and what remains is just pure experience—no story, no identification with subject, object, "I," or "other." This is also the definition of presence, and for those few months, wherever I

went and whatever I did, it seemed presence stalked me. I picked
up an apple in the grocery store and I *was* the apple—that is, I
was not aware of myself as something separate from the experience of apple. I went for a walk in the mountains, looked down
to observe my steps, one foot in front of the other, and I *became*
the walking. Eventually, I got behind the wheel of a motor vehicle; my hand put the key in the ignition and I was at once the
hand, the key, the engine rumbling. One long series of bizarre
moments strung together for approximately three months. Later
I'd learn that I'd experienced what Buddhism would describe
as no separation: the experience of joining with or becoming
one with whatever arises. Despite what my conditioning told
me, despite what I thought to be real, I knew in those moments
that I was not an entity that existed separate from what I experienced. Presence wasn't stalking me; I *was* present.

This extraordinary occurrence diminished over time, but the
feeling stayed with me. I saw that if I had enough free attention to cut through my habituated patterns and fears, I could
be present in my life, otherwise I couldn't. Simple concept, difficult to execute. But this awareness allowed me to see the world
and myself through a different lens. It would shift the way I
worked, the way I operated in relationships, even the way I managed my health issues—which, by the way, had not disappeared
but merely mutated. It would also prompt me to find a Buddhist teacher with whom to study. But that all came later. First
I decided to spend a couple of months at my parents' house in
the country—a period of reentry, so to speak, a time to integrate the journey.

Two months turned into nearly two years of isolation and
meditation and writing the story of my passage. For the most
part I did not go out or visit with friends or think about the
future. I did go on several extended silent meditation retreats in

which I was able to deepen my awareness practice. I even thought about entering the monastery, but I wasn't about to force the answers. If I'd learned anything while away, it was how to trust. My not knowing bothered my parents more than it bothered me, but they were willing to suspend judgment and allow me to do what I needed to do, even if what I needed to do seemed foreign. Occasionally, my stepfather would ask, "So, how much longer do you need? How about cutting it off at the end of the year?" And I would nod silently in agreement, even though I had no idea how much time was needed or where I'd be at the end of the year.

Then something curious happened. My isolation ended. I awoke early one morning to the rooster's crowing, the sky a pale blue. I went on a long hike, sat for hours on the beach, thought, reflected. I came home, picked up the phone, and called my ex-fiancé, Todd, who was living in San Francisco.

"Hi, it's Jess," I said.

Todd and I had kept in touch via email, so I knew generally what was going on in his life: he'd moved up north, started a new job, seemed happy. "Hey, stranger," he said. "How are you? How's the transition back?"

"Okay." I paused before I spoke again. "I'd like to come see you."

"Oh." This time it was he who paused. "What's up?"

"I thought maybe we could talk."

"What about?"

"About us, about getting back together." The words came out like the notion was the most natural thing in the world.

"What? Jess, this is sort of out of left field, don't you think? Why now? I mean after all this time?"

I'd thrown him for a loop and I knew he'd need time to digest the conversation. "Let's talk about it when I get there."

I flew up to San Francisco for a weekend of questions and answers. I did my best to explain why I'd needed to go away, why he couldn't visit, and how the journey had changed me. "It was a rite of passage, really, a sort of quest."

"A quest for what?"

"Peace, maybe. A better understanding of myself, of how things work."

"Did you find what you were looking for?"

"I did."

"What makes you think this won't happen again, you won't wake up one day feeling stuck and want to take off?" he asked.

It was a fair question. "I'm pretty sure it was a one-time event. I've given this a lot of thought, I've even considered remaining single, perhaps entering the monastery, but I've known and loved you for fifteen years and I can't imagine growing old without you. I believe I can do both—be in a relationship and remain committed to my path."

"I hope you're right," he said.

And just like that I reentered mainstream life.

Todd and I spent the next several months getting reacquainted. He'd recently been let go from his job, another casualty of corporate downsizing, so we had a rare and unprecedented opportunity to tend to our relationship. I honestly don't know if we could have gotten things back on track had we not been given that precious window of time. Eventually he was offered a new position in Los Angeles, and suddenly we were buying a house and planning to get married. Outwardly, my life looked much as it had before I went to Central America; inwardly everything was different. I'd let go of my desire to attain enlightenment, to become wise or compassionate or powerful. My intention was simply to be present in my life, to remember that I was not separate from what I experienced, and to be awake in each moment. I knew that was all I had.

And so, on a warm July night in 2002, two and a half years after I returned from Central America and nearly five years after we'd broken our engagement, Sanda married Todd and me in my parents' backyard, encircled by horses and pheasants, an African drummer, and a small cluster of family and friends.

And the journey continues.

Acknowledgments

This book would not have come to life without the guidance and support of Andrea Cagan, author, editor, and writing mentor extraordinaire. During weekly phone sessions, Andrea helped me transform four lengthy journals into a legitimate first draft, then a second, until eventually I had the confidence to continue on my own. I am grateful to Sherry Lansing and Mitchell Ivers for reading the original journals and for introducing me to Andrea; birthing this book was made tolerable, at times even joyful, because of her.

But I never would have made it through the journey to write this book had it not been for Sanda Jasper. By opening her heart and sharing her wisdom, Sanda helped ready me for the pilgrimage to Central America and graciously made herself accessible by phone whenever I was in trouble or doubted my ability to continue. Her integrity as a teacher and her faith in the process of awakening are exquisite and inspiring and I am forever grateful.

I am indebted to my mother and stepfather for many things, but particularly for allowing me to hole up in their spare room for the two years it took to write this book and transition back into the fold. Thank you for letting me go and letting me be.

There are many others who directly and indirectly supported my efforts to complete this ridiculously long project: Peri Doslu, Victoria Charles, Kristin Hahn, Andy Cohen, Kay Garrett, Katherine Boyle, Hal and Linda Kramer, Roger Jellinek and Eden-Lee Murray, Reverend Michael Beckwith, Tanya Christensen, Ken McLeod, and my entire family. Thank you all for your unique and soulful contributions.

And finally, my heartfelt gratitude to my husband, Todd, for everything else.

Resources

*Agape International
Center of Truth*
5700 Buckingham Parkway
Culver City, CA 90230
310.348.1250
Agapelive.com

Cross Cultural Journeys
PO Box 1369
Sausalito, CA 94966
800.353.2276
CrossCulturalJourneys.com

*Dance of the Deer Foundation
Center for Shamanic Studies*
PO Box 699
Sequel, CA 95073
831.475.9560
Shamanism.com

Esalen Institute
Highway 1
Big Sur, CA 93920
831.667.3000
Esalen.org

Foundation for
Shamanic Studies
PO Box 2939
Mill Valley, CA 94942
415.380.8282
ShamanicStudies.com

Inquiring Mind Newsletter
PO Box 9999
Berkeley, CA 94709
Inquiringmind.org

Insight Meditation Society and Forest Refuge
1230 Pleasant Street
Barre, MA 01005
800.641.1983
Dharma.org

Institute of Noetic Sciences
101 San Antonio Road
Petaluma, CA 94952
707.775.3500
Noetic.org

Osani Holistic Health Care
15113 Sunset Blvd.
Pacific Palisades, CA 90272
310.454.4427
Osani@earthlink.net

The Ojai Foundation
9739 Ojai-Santa Paula Rd.
Ojai, CA 93023
805.646.8343
OjaiFoundation.org

Sounds True Catalogue
PO Box 8010
Boulder, CO 80306
800.333.9185
Soundstrue.com

Spirit Rock Meditation Center
PO Box 169
Woodacre, CA 94973
415.488.0164
Spiritrock.org

Unfettered Mind
13323 Washington Blvd., Suite 302
Los Angeles CA 90066
310.827.7766
Unfetteredmind.org

What Is Enlightenment?
PO Box 2360
Lenox, MA 01240
USA: 800.376.3210
Europe: 44.207.419.8100
WhatIsEnlightenment.org

Yoga Journal
2054 University Ave., Suite 600
Berkeley, CA 94704
1.800.600.YOGA
YogaJournal.com

About the Author

Jessica Nagler is a writer, psychotherapist, and former adjunct faculty member at Pepperdine University. An eating disorders specialist, she has worked in residential treatment facilities and privately. Jessica has been published in the *LA Daily Journal* and the *LA Therapist Update*. She and her husband live in Los Angeles, where she offers psychotherapy, spiritual counseling, and mindfulness training.

For more information on Jessica Nagler's work, or to give feedback to the author, please visit her online at www.jessicanagler.com.